D0095365

HOW TO MINISTER TO SENIOR ADULTS
IN YOUR CHURCH

HOW TO MINISTER TO
Senior Adults
IN YOUR CHURCH

HORACE L. KERR

BROADMAN PRESS
Nashville, Tennessee

Dewey Decimal Classification: 259

Subject heading: CHURCH WORK WITH SENIOR ADULTS

Library of Congress Catalog Card Number: 77-80944

Printed in the United States of America

"I am come that they might have life, and that they might have it more abundantly" (John 10:10b).

THIS BOOK IS DEDICATED TO:

All who serve to assure that abundant life for the millions of senior adults in our churches and communities,

all with whom I have been associated personally and professionally who have contributed to my own development, and

my wife, children, and grandchildren, who continue to provide joy and meaning to my own life as I grow older.

FOREWORD

Earliest recorded history reveals that man has always been preoccupied with increasing the longevity of life. All literature, from Genesis to the mountain of present-day writings, has reflected this interest. As a result, a large body of knowledge has evolved out of a study of aging and related concerns. However, subjects of prime importance have been largely neglected. They have to do with the church — her role, her need to be involved, and the development of a ministry to meet some of the needs of the elderly. Horace Kerr has written this book to supplement the limited resources available in these areas. It combines the *what* and *why* with a practical step-by-step guide for developing a ministry with older persons in a local church.

Many books have been written beyond the experience of their authors. I would like to assure the readers that this volume was born out of the author's major vocational experiences that span nearly thirty years. These were tasks vitally related to ministry and service to senior adults. As an administrator and minister of education, he served in churches for twenty years — thirteen of these years with First Baptist Church, Jackson, Mississippi. In this strategic church, he developed special programs for senior adults, while working with them through the more traditional organizations. Ministry in this downtown church with thousands of members and prospects, including a high percentage of senior adults, provided varied and rich experiences.

The governor of Mississippi, aware of the author's expertise, experience, and leadership, selected him as the executive director of the Mississippi Council on Aging. This agency of the state was assigned the main responsibility for advocacy for 330,000 senior adults in Mississippi. During his five years of leadership in this key position, Kerr initiated the development of strategically located area agencies on aging over the entire state. Through these agencies, hundreds of field workers, thousands of volunteers, and a strong central staff, he was instrumental in providing or enhancing almost every conceivable type of service for senior adults. Elderly day care; information and referral; transportation; group and home delivered meals; R.S.V.P.; Foster Grandparents; senior aides; home health care; employment services; leadership training for nursing home workers, ministers, and other professionals; and a host of other services proliferated under his capable leadership.

The author is presently leading the senior adult ministry program in the Family Ministry Department of the Sunday School Board of the Southern Baptist Convention. This position has afforded him an exceptional vantage point in surveying and studying model programs in churches across the United States.

Thus, the author's vocational pilgrimage reflects a leading that is beyond human design. It is as though he has been destined and prepared for the noble work of helping to make life increasingly abundant for those in their senior years. Formal education through multiplied conferences, seminars, and consultations were an integral part of his vocational tasks. Clinical and classroom experiences were blended in the midst of the important work of each day. One of his outstanding classroom experiences was at the Percy Andrus Gerontology Center at the University of Southern California, a center in the forefront of gerontological research. His undergraduate studies were focused on sociology, with studies at the masters' level culminating in the Master of Religious Education degree. Later, the Juris Doctor degree marked another level of academic achievement.

Kerr has written several articles for sectarian and nonsectarian publications and served as a consultant for the National Interfaith Coalition on Aging, of which he is a member. He also holds membership in the following organizations: The Gerontological Society, National Council on the Aging, American Association of Retired Persons, and the Southern Baptist Association of Ministries with the Aging.

Out of this unique and substantial background, the author shares proven, practical suggestions, information, and instructions with the purpose of improving and enlarging ministries for and with senior adults in the church. On more than one occasion over the years, I have heard experienced workers in the field of aging say: "Listen closely when Horace Kerr speaks. Each word is important!" This book is the outgrowth of a rare combination of vocational experience, education, and dedication. Read it carefully!

CARROLL B. FREEMAN
Professor, Psychology and Counseling
New Orleans Baptist Theological Seminary
June 1979

PREFACE

Interest in the field of aging and in older persons themselves has captivated the attention of the world. Books of all shapes and sizes have been published on the subject. A few have concentrated on the church and its role, its need to be involved, and how it can meet some of the needs of the elderly. My purpose is not to merely add another volume on the subject.

In a 1975 project, the Research Department of The Sunday School Board of the Southern Baptist Convention asked churches what assistance for senior adult work was needed from the denomination. Fifty-one percent replied they saw a need for motivational plans and promotion. Forty-two percent asked for assistance in organization and planning. Forty percent indicated a need for leadership training. My search of available literature has revealed a need for a book which combines the *what* and *why* with a practical step-by-step guide for developing a ministry with older persons in a local church.

The Senior Adult Ministry Section of the Family Ministry Department was formed by The Sunday School Board of the Southern Baptist Convention in 1975 to serve the needs as indicated from the results of a survey. We offer guidance, training, and materials to the more than 35,000 Southern Baptist churches and others in their ministry to and with senior adults. We also provide special activities and materials for senior adults themselves. Our objectives are:

1. To create an awareness of the presence and the potential of senior adults.

2. To provide for a better understanding of the aging process.

3. To assist Baptist state conventions, regional associations, and churches to meet the needs of senior adults in the areas of spiritual

enrichment, social interaction, meaningful service opportunities, learning opportunities, and special services for those who need them.

4. To provide fellowship opportunities on a nationwide basis through conferences, cruises and tours, and a national membership organization.

5. To work with other departments and agencies to provide a comprehensive system of programming for and with senior adults.

In 1976 we introduced a leisure-reading, large-print magazine, *Mature Living.* As of this writing, *Mature Living* has developed a circulation of more than 180,000. We have also established an organization called the National Association of Baptist Senior Adults; its membership exceeds 25,000. Because of the immediate success of the magazine, we have also embarked on an aggressive book publishing venture. Several book titles, which will be referred to later, for both senior adults and leaders are available from Broadman Press and Convention Press. Chautauquas, which were begun in 1972, accommodate approximately 6,000 persons per year. These are conferences for senior adults and their leaders held at Southern Baptist Conference Centers in North Carolina and New Mexico. Planning and leadership are provided for in numerous conferences and workshops throughout the nation.

Through these experiences we have gained much information on the needs and interests of senior adults. We have witnessed a variety of approaches that churches use to meet those needs and have had opportunities to evaluate those methods. From this background, I have written this book to provide information, suggestions, and instructions for the purpose of improved and enlarged ministries with and to senior adults in your church. There are frequent references to "you" as the person responsible for certain actions. Most often the responsibility is that of the Senior Adult Coordinator; but you, the reader, may want to see that the actions are accomplished.

I am indebted to Dr. Frank E. Cotton, Department of Industrial Engineering, Mississippi State University, for many of the concepts included in chapter 3. They were set forth in a manual entitled *Planning For the Aging,* © Frank E. Cotton, Jr., 1975, which he prepared for the Mississippi Council on Aging. This material is used with his permission.

HORACE L. KERR

CONTENTS

PART I
A Rationale for Ministry

1
Senior Adults: Who Are They?

Senior Adults: Who Are They?

As you consider a program of ministry with senior adults, it is important that you understand who senior adults really are, what they are really like. There is so much misinformation and so many myths. In my experience I have found many people who believe that older people are incapable of learning, reject anything new, are sick, complain constantly, are of little value to society, are doomed to senility, and should accept passively their lot as persons disengaged from work and society. What do you think? That image is not consistent with reality. Research and surveys reveal aging in a much more acceptable light, both for those who are elderly now and for those of us who will likely be old someday.

Are You Prejudiced?

Walk with me along a busy street. See that elderly woman hesitating as she crosses the street? Others almost bump into her as they hurry in both directions. Cars must stop before turning into the intersection. The light changes before she is safely on the opposite sidewalk; other cars must wait.

What emotions fill that scene? Irritation? Impatience? Anger? Disgust? Pity? Fear? Embarrassment? Understanding? What do you feel? Do such incidents color how you feel about *all* older persons?

A friend retired several years ago as executive secretary of an important agency. Later he served twice as director of a small school for handicapped children. He has been a recognized leader in civic affairs. He has served his church in many capacities through the years. He is still active and eager to serve. But what about the younger men? Should he step aside and let them have their turn? He has served long and well. Should he now be content to rest and let others do for him? How do you feel? Does it color how you feel about all older persons?

Ageism, the attitude and practice which demeans older persons, supports unjust stereotyping. Ageism is seen often in the portrayal of older adults in the media, especially the entertainment field. It is reflected in written and spoken comments on old age. It often results in frequent discrimination against the elderly. Such prejudice may be reflected in the self-concept of some senior adults. They may not feel comfortable being themselves, even when they know they don't feel, look, or act like the stereotype.

No Stereotypes

No common denominator other than age can truly be applied to those in their senior years. We use phrases like "old (or young) for one's age" or "second childhood" to describe those who do not fit the mold of expected behavior for their chronological age. We often ask "How old is he?" with the expectation of learning much about that person. Actually, we will only know how many years he has lived!

Nowhere is the practice of stereotyping less valid than in the senior years. Stereotyping categorizes persons as having so many similarities that they are "all" alike—predictable as to thought and actions.

As one ages, he becomes more himself, more of an individual. He is more different from his peers than at any earlier time. It is not as important to him that he conform in appearance, thought, or action. He is the result of the specific physical, emotional, and environmental circumstances of his own existence. His many experiences have contributed to make him who he is and cause him to think and act as he does.

Of course, it is a sociological fact that those born during the same period—say, of ten years—do have similar experiences which may influence all of them. For example, the psychological impact on

DIVERSE

those in the labor force during the great depression of the 1930s has resulted in many of them demonstrating a cautious conservativism.

"Train up a child in the way he should go: and when he is old, he will not depart from it" (Prov. 22:6) speaks to this principle of individuality. This principle operates throughout a person's life as he shapes his own future. So some senior adults are happy—others are sad;

  some are physically strong—others are not well;

  some are economically poor—others are wealthy;

  some are pessimistic—others are optimistic;

  some are highly active—others are more sedate;

  some are demanding—others are quietly withdrawn;

  some are independent—others need and accept help;

  some are well educated—others have little formal education.

The list of opposites could go on, but the point is: Senior adults are diverse.

True Perspectives

Unfortunately, a popular view of old age is a stereotype supported by early studies done in institutional settings. It is the picture of a stooped, gray, wrinkled, shuffling, sick, complaining, dependent, socially unaccepted *old* person. You have only to look about you to see that this is not the portrait of all persons in their retirement years. In fact, that image would portray a very small percentage. According to a 1978 publication by the United States Department of Health, Education, and Welfare, only 4 percent of persons over age 65 lived in any kind of institution in 1977. Another 10 to 15 percent may require varying kinds and degrees of assistance. So fully 80 to 85 percent of senior adults are able to manage their own everyday affairs.

To have a true perspective of aging, you must accept the process as normal and universal, but varying with the individual. A developmental process is at work throughout a person's life from conception, when he begins to be formed physically, until death. We were all born, and we shall all die. In between, we *age*.

This developmental process is commonly understood and accepted through the early stages of growth and maturation to adulthood. More often the terminology changes at that point, and the continuing process is referred to as "aging." When we realize that a person develops in reaction to physiological, psychological, sociological, and spiritual forces, we can understand that this developmental process is lifelong. In fact, it is the process of living.

This process is *sequential, cumulative,* and *irreversible.*

It is *sequential* in that everyone must develop through the stages of life in the same order: infancy, childhood, youth, adulthood, older adulthood. No one skips a stage. Every person progresses through the stages at his own pace. Therefore, delineating the stages by chronological ages is not possible.

The process is *cumulative* in that what one becomes, learns, and experiences at one stage is carried to the next stage. So in a sense, we are fashioned by our past.

For example, persons' experiences in the 1930s have an impact on them even now. I am not espousing a fatalistic approach to life; indeed, we are able to change and overcome circumstances. However, the cumulative nature of one's development does have significant impact. This factor is helpful in understanding attitudes and actions.

Finally, this process is *irreversible.* Nicodemus was right when he stated that no man can return to his mother's womb to be born again physically (John 3:4). There is no second childhood! Persons can only demonstrate childlike behavior—which is not acceptable in later stages of development. The process is continuing, upward. We can't go back; nor, in fact, do most people want to go back to a former stage of life.

God's Creation

Who are senior adults? Perhaps the most important answer to that question is: They are God's creation. "God created man in his own image, in the image of God created he him; male and female created he them" (Gen. 1:27). The first man was apparently created an adult, but the "image of God" characteristic does not appear to be age-related. Man is in the image of God throughout his entire life. The older, wrinkled face topped by gray or sparse hair and supported by a weakened body is no less the image of God than the younger, firmer face crowned by dark hair and supported by a virile, strong body. Spiritually and mentally, the older person may well be more in the image of God than a younger person because the multiplied experiences of a longer life can add to one's understanding and acceptance of God. God has purposes for all of his creation. His promises are not limited by age. One does not retire from belonging to him.

Worth and Purpose

Senior adults are persons of worth, not only as God's creation, but also for what they have done, what they can do, and—more importantly—for who they are. Many of the institutions and conveniences we enjoy today were provided by those who are now retired. Leadership, wisdom, and service compose the continuing potential of our older citizens. They have arrived at a stage in life where they can be themselves without the need for or limitations of supporting job titles. They have worth in themselves!

There is purpose in all of life. We see it readily in the young as they prepare for adult responsibilities. Formation of families, propagation of the population, production of goods and services—all are accepted as purposes of adulthood until retirement. So what are the purposes of the later years? Here are some suggestions; surely there are others.

1. The later years provide one's only real opportunity to become oneself. We live in a future-oriented society which places a premium on doing and achieving. In his book *Learn to Grow Old*, Paul Tournier emphasizes the importance of one's turning from the conformity of vocational life to pursue his own human fulfillment in his retirement years. With the reduced restraints of schedule, image, and responsibility, he can for the first time do what he wants to do, when he wants to do it, the way he wants to do it. He is free to be himself.

2. Older persons provide a balance to society. This purpose recognizes a continuing responsibility and wisdom which can come only from having lived a long time. As a friend puts it, "If it weren't for the older people in this country, there wouldn't be enough sense to run it!" Certainly, there is need for the energetic enthusiasm of youth, but there is also the need for tempering by the aged.

3.   3. Lengthened life also provides one with previously unrealized opportunities for personal development. Prior to retirement, much of a person's formal and continuing education has been preparation for further education and/or enhancement of vocation. Now an older person may engage in learning just for the sake of learning.

4   4. Spiritual growth may well be at its highest in the later years of life. Certainly, the experiences of life provide more potential for understanding God and the teachings of his Word. With more control over the use of time in retirement, a person can give more time to Bible study and meditation. As the Christian ages, he becomes more reflective and can see the moving hand of God throughout his life. Such memories add confidence and strength for the future.

5   5. The senior years offer one his greatest opportunity to serve others. The freedom of time allows the senior adult the opportunity to give more to personal services. Some may continue the kinds of service they gave in preretirement days.

Two retired pastors with whom I worked still spend much of their time visiting the lonely, the sick, and the bereaved. Another friend says she is enjoying being a neighbor to those who live nearby; she was barely acquainted with them before she retired from a professional position in her denomination. A retired librarian and her husband, a retired bookkeeper, and a retired housekeeper and her husband are among those who have responded to needs for short-term volunteer service in foreign missions. Others have contributed their time and skills to their local churches, the community in which they live, and other worthwhile causes. Mainly retirees find opportunities to provide natural support to persons in need, without fanfare or organizational structures. The reward for the senior adult is the satisfaction of continuing usefulness and meaning in life from service to others, a real fulfillment in the later years.

Needs

The basic needs of persons are no less real in later life than earlier. The needs of senior adults differ more in degree than in kind from those of other ages. Psychologist Abraham Maslow ranks human needs in the order he believes they must be met from lower to higher as shown in this chart.

ABRAHAM MASLOW'S HIERARCHY OF NEEDS

H
i
g
h
e
r

Need for
SELF-ACTUALIZATION

To develop to one's fullest capacity as a human being; to find

O meaning in life; to find answers to life's questions.

r
d
e
r

ESTEEM NEEDS

Sense of adequacy, of competence, of achievement, of contribution; recognition, prestige.

L
o
BELONGINGNESS AND LOVE NEEDS w
The need for affection, inclusion, place in one's group. e
r

SAFETY NEEDS

O
Security, protection against physical threats; familiarity and r
stability of the environment. d
e
r

PHYSIOLOGICAL NEEDS
For food, housing, clothing, health care, mobility.

Health, security, love, esteem, and self-fulfillment are concerns for all of life.

The reality of special needs in later life is obvious. For example, many live alone in virtual isolation with little opportunity of being with others. They are not challenged by meaning in their lives. With reduced motivation, they likely practice poor nutrition habits and get little physical exercise. These would have needs most younger persons would not experience.

Others lose their sense of purpose in life as they retire from what they've been *doing* vocationally. Their vocations have been almost tantamount to what they have *been,* according to our practice of labeling persons by what they do—secretary, salesman, preacher, nurse, housewife, mechanic, lawyer, laborer. Many retired persons have difficulty explaining who they are when the vocation labels no longer fit. Those same persons may have difficulty experiencing meaning in their lives and feeling good about themselves when they give up the vocational descriptive labels. Such persons may have needs for acceptance, self-esteem, and fulfillment to a greater degree than ever before.

Some senior adults begin to doubt God's promises and their relationship to him when life does not fulfill their expectations. They may be so entrenched in the Protestant Work Ethic (which in essence states that every man should earn his own bread) that they feel guilty in not being engaged in the work force. They may also be holding on to the Old Testament philosophy that if things are not going right, then their relationships with God must not be right. Senior adults need proper understanding and assurance of God's promises.

The Losses of Old Age

Old age has been characterized by loss—physical, economic, status, role, family, spouse, friends, home, freedom. It is not my primary purpose in this book to provide a detailed discussion of these losses, or of all the needs of senior adults. The bibliography in the Appendix suggests many written and audio resources which will be helpful at this point. I recommend highly *The Senior Adult Years: A Christian Psychology of Aging* by Dr. Carroll B. Freeman (see Bibliography). However, some elaboration will be helpful here.

There is an obvious loss of physical strength as one ages. This process is normal. Statistically, however, fully 80 to 85 percent of all senior adults are physically capable of meeting their own daily requirements. All five senses tend to lose efficiency as one ages. This process should also be recognized as normal. Incidentally, the process of decline in sensory acuity does not begin at age 65. Many adults begin to have some difficulty with vision at about age 40. Hearing losses may occur in the middle adult years. The senses of smell, taste, and touch may not be affected until later.

Most retirees incur economic loss. Many retire on half or even less than half of their previous incomes. Those who are retired on fixed incomes, of course, have been severely affected by rampant inflation. Although most retired persons do not have financial needs which are as great as before, the lack of money is still a problem.

Loss of status and role related to one's occupation is often traumatic, especially to those who have not anticipated that possibility and prepared themselves for it. Of course, status and role may be attained by persons apart from their vocations. The need here is for a person to make that discovery and to appropriate it for himself.

Loss of significant others — friends, family, spouse — occurs as one grows older. This loss emphasizes the need for continuing to develop new relationships while maintaining and enriching old relationships throughout one's life.

For some, the need will come to seek alternative housing and possible physical care which will require giving up one's home. Some measure of freedom may be lost in such a change. For those who suffer severe physical losses, there is even a greater degree of loss of freedom. Keep in mind that though those experiencing such physical loss may be a large number, they will probably total no more than 15 percent of the total senior adult population.

Senior adults' losses and needs should be evident even in this brief description. But this is only the negative side of aging. This information serves only to demonstrate the need for compensating actions by the senior adult himself and by those who care, if there is to be life with dignity, meaning, and satisfaction.

Capabilities

These are adults — *senior* adults! They are grown persons who have developed capacities and skills through years of experience. They know what they like. They can think and choose for themselves. Making decisions is not new to them. New and challenging experiences have always been a part of their lives. They now face still another pioneer experience — that of living in retirement.

The generations now retired are the first of any significant numbers to be so classified. When the Social Security Act was passed in 1935, life expectancy at birth was about 63 years. This plan was to provide financial assistance to the relatively few who would live beyond the arbitrary 65 years of age set for the cessation from active labor. No other apparent consideration was given to the establishment of a role for those to be retired. Society had not arrived at an expectation model for such a group, as it had for other stages of life.

By 1970 we experienced a retirement boom with more people living to and beyond age 65. This segment of twenty million (nearly 10 percent of the total population) was indeed pioneering in an uncharted social phenomenon. But when we consider the many socioeconomic changes successfully faced in the lifetime of these older citizens, there is no reason for us to think, or to encourage them to think, that they cannot now cope with the pioneer experience of the retirement years. That is not to say that we should leave senior adults to shift for themselves. Rather, we must emphasize that they should not be made dependent on the designs of others. They must be allowed and encouraged to participate in — indeed, to lead in — the development of their new role in society.

Definition

This segment of our society has been given a variety of labels: *senior citizens, golden agers, the elderly, older Americans, older persons. Senior adults* is the term used here. A group of professional church and denomination workers, representing various church programs, selected this term as more appropriate to the elderly than any other term considered. The term connotes dignity, while identifying the group. These persons are adults, and they are the seniors of their age group. *Older persons* or *the elderly* are synonyms which will also be used here. Some may feel that these are more appropriate terms because they are direct. I, too, feel that we should use terms which do not gloss over reality.

Various ages are used to designate the beginning point for this period of life. Most retirement plans use 65. The Social Security Act recognizes 62 as a possibility. The United States Older American Act programs are available to persons age 60 and over. The American Association of Retired Persons accepts members at age 55. The United States Department of Labor defines an older worker as one who has reached his 45th birthday. The focus of the concerns and programs detailed in this book is on those who are retired from their major vocation. That includes work outside or inside the home—whether or not salary was earned. This definition also includes the semiretired. If an age needs to be suggested, then it would be age 60, qualified to include younger retired persons and to recognize that not all 60-year-olds will be ready for such programs. Age 60 does appear to be a more appropriate beginning point because of earlier retirement trends and because of the needs and interests of women not employed outside the home whose children no longer consume their time and attention.

Senior adults, then, are defined here as those persons who are in their retirement years.

Summary

Senior adults are persons. They are a large segment of our population today. One in seven, 28,000,000, are age 60 or older. As a group they are relatively new on our scene.

We must be aware of their potential and interested in each individual continuing to advance "unto the measure of the stature of the fulness of Christ" (Eph. 4:13).

2

Senior Adult Ministry: Responsibility and Opportunity for the Church

The pastor of a large church said, "The older people in my church are beginning to expect as much from the church as the young people. They even want to do many of the same things, such as go on trips and have fellowship periods." Surprise and questions were obvious in the tone of his voice. I have heard the same reaction many times.

What is the responsibility of the church in providing for senior adults? To what extent should a church go? What special opportunities does the church have as it relates to the elderly?

Responsibility for All Persons

The church has an obligation to aid all persons—whatever their stage of development—to achieve their fullest potential as persons responsible to God and to their fellowman. In the context of this obligation, neglecting senior adults would be unthinkable for two reasons. First, even though one might have lived a long time, no one ever reaches that state of perfection. Second, senior adults can continue to grow.

Biblical Teachings on Aging

The Bible contains many references to age and the aged which emphasize the importance of this group. The Old Testament declares that longevity of life is a special *blessing of God*: "And if thou wilt walk in my ways, to keep my statutes and my commandments, as thy father David did walk, then I will lengthen thy days" (1 Kings 3:14).

Older persons are *deserving of honor, respect and recognition*: "Honour thy father and thy mother: that thy days may be long upon the land which the Lord God giveth thee" (Ex. 20:12). "Thou shalt rise up before the hoary head, and honour the face of the old man, and fear thy God: I am the Lord" (Lev. 19:32). "Hearken unto thy father that begat thee, and despise not thy mother when she is old" (Prov. 23:22). "Cast me not off in the time of old age; forsake me not when my strength faileth" (Ps. 71:9).

Wisdom and maturity generally accompany old age: "With the ancient is wisdom; and in length of days understanding" (Job 12:12). "Remember the days of old, consider the years of many generations: Ask thy father, and he will show thee; thy elders, and they will tell thee" (Deut. 32:7).

Old age is a *normal part of life*: "To everything there is a season, and a time to every purpose under the heaven: A time to be born, and a time to die" (Eccl. 3:1-2a). "The days of our years are three-score years and ten; and if by reason of strength they be fourscore years, yet is there strength labor and sorrow; for it is soon cut off, and we fly away. O satisfy us early with thy mercy; that we may rejoice and be glad all our days" (Ps. 90:10,14).

The latter years of one's life are a *time of fulfillment of promises* and the receiving of rewards: "And even to your old age I am he; and even to hoar hairs will I carry you: I have made, and I will bear; even I will carry, and will deliver you" (Isa. 46:4). "They shall not build, and another inhabit; they shall not plant, and another eat: for as the days of a tree are the days of my people, and mine elect shall long enjoy the work of their hands" (Isa. 65:22).

In the New Testament *Jesus emphasized persons* without regard to sex, age, nationality, or station in life. He said, "For *whosoever* shall do the will of my Father which is in heaven, the same is my brother, and sister, and mother" (Matt. 12:50). On another occasion he said, "And him that cometh to me I will in no wise cast out" (John 6:37b). The fact that Jesus gave his life for individuals is proof of the value he places on persons. In the book of Acts and some of the epistles we do find references to the aged.

There is the continuing emphasis on *respect for the elderly*: "Rebuke not an elder, but entreat him as a father; and the younger men as brethren; the elder women as mothers; the younger as sisters, with all purity" (1 Tim. 5:1-2).

Older persons are to *set an example for and to teach the younger*: "But speak thou the things which become sound doctrine: that the aged men be sober, grave, temperate, sound in faith, in charity, in patience. The aged women likewise, that they be in behaviour as becometh holiness, not false accusers, not given to much wine, teachers of good things; that they may teach the young women to be sober, to love their husbands, to love their children, to be discreet, chaste, keepers at home, good, obedient to their own husbands, that the word of God be not blasphemed. Young men likewise exhort to be sober minded. In all things showing thyself a pattern of good works: in doctrine showing uncorruptness, gravity, sincerity, sound speech, that cannot be condemned; that he that is of the contrary part may be ashamed, having no evil thing to say of you" (Titus 2:1-8).

"The elders which are among you I exhort, who am also an elder, and a witness of the sufferings of Christ, and also a partaker of the glory that shall be revealed: Feed the flock of God which is among you, asking the oversight thereof, not by constraint, but willingly; not for filthy lucre, but of a ready mind; neither as being lords over God's heritage, but being ensamples to the flock" (1 Pet. 5:1-5).

There is also *implication for care* being provided the elderly as reference is made to widows: "Pure religion and undefiled before God and the Father is this, To visit the fatherless and widows in their affliction, and to keep himself unspotted from the world" (Jas. 1:27). The selection of the first deacons was occasioned by the need to minister to widows (Acts 6:1-7).

Many *promises* have special meaning for older persons: "I am come that they might have life, and that they might have it more abundantly" (John 10:10b). "Therefore, my beloved brethren, be ye stedfast, unmoveable, always abounding in the work of the Lord, forasmuch as ye know that your labour is not in vain in the Lord" (1 Cor. 15:58). "But the fruit of the Spirit is love, joy, peace, long suffering, gentleness, goodness, faith, meekness, temperance: against such there is no law" (Gal. 5:22-23).

The *exhortations to strive for excellence* in Christ certainly knows no age limits: "And he gave some, apostles; and some, prophets; and some, evangelists; and some, pastors and teachers; for the perfecting of the saints, for the work of the ministry, for the edifying of the body of Christ: till we all come in the unity of the faith, and of the knowledge of the Son of God, unto a perfect man, unto the measure of the stature of the fulness of Christ" (Eph. 4:11-13). "I press toward the mark for the prize of the high calling of God in Christ Jesus" (Phil. 3:14). "But grow in grace, and in the knowledge of our Lord and Saviour Jesus Christ. To him be glory both now and for ever. Amen" (2 Pet. 3:18).

Responsibility for Senior Adults

Senior adult ministry as used here includes *all the church does and can do to make life meaningful and a growing experience for older persons in its membership and community.* It is a comprehensive program to meet many of the real needs of senior adults.

The premise on which this book is developed is that there are five content areas the church should consider in a ministry with senior adults. They are: spiritual enrichment, learning opportunities, socialization, service opportunities, and services needed. These areas cover comprehensively the needs of senior adults as discussed in chapter 1. They speak especially to the three highest levels in Maslow's hierarchy of needs. They are also appropriate to the generally conceived role of a church when compared with roles of other community organizations.

Here are some ways the local church can serve the needs of senior adults:

• A church interprets and assists in achieving the abundant life which Jesus came to give (John 10:10b). It begins when one becomes a Christian and grows as he experiences Christ's presence throughout life. The church pronounces the joy of assurance of God's mercy and providence. (Unlike happiness, joy can be real whatever one's circumstances.)

• The church demonstrates God's mercy as it shows interest, concern, and care for each member and others, including the elderly. Galatians 6:2 teaches that we fulfill the law of Christ when we bear one another's burdens. Jesus himself declared (Matt. 25:40) that as we minister to the needs of others we minister to him. In Romans 15:1 the strong are instructed to bear the infirmities of the weak.

• A church is God's agent for bringing about right attitudes. (Jesus began his Sermon on the Mount with statements of right attitudes for his followers, as Matt. 5:2-12 relates.) Often the negative attitude of the older person as well as that of society causes him to think less of himself than he should. We need to destroy the myths of aging, retirement, and old age. A church by its nature has opportunities to do that.

• A church fellowship provides both spiritual and social enrichment. Both are vital to the aging person as he experiences retirement, increased leisure, loss of friends, loss of family, loss of health, decreased income, and possibly loss of purpose. God's Word and his people can best provide assurance and encouragement needed by senior adults.

• A church requires the best efforts of its leadership in programming, planning, and administration. Senior adults with their mental strength — their accumulation of knowledge and wisdom — should be utilized in the decision-making process. They also have the skills to perform major business and administration tasks. When older persons are used, the church benefits, and the elderly have their needs met.

• A church uses the abilities of its members to accomplish its purposes. The talents and time of senior adults can be utilized in meaningful service opportunities in and through the church. Ten percent of senior adults surveyed by the Harris Poll in 1975 for the National Council on Aging indicated that they would like to serve as volunteers. Added to the 22 percent already in volunteer jobs, that would indicate a ready work force for many of the tasks of the churches. To achieve self-esteem one needs to be needed.

• A ministry with senior adults is an opportunity to support the families of the church. Families face new relationships and concerns as more persons live to experience retirement. Most have a life expectancy of sixteen years beyond age 65. This has produced what some are calling the *sandwich generation*: middle-aged adults, who have some responsibility for their parents at the same time their children and spouses need them the most. A more recent phenomenon is the aged parent who is cared for by children who are also retired. The shifting independent-dependent role is difficult for both and may well affect all members of the family.

Opportunities are needed for multigeneration interaction. This need may best be provided through the church as a type of family. Changes occur within the nuclear family (husband, wife, children) when:

children move away;

retirement brings a full-time home relationship for husband and wife;

failing health adds responsibility for care;

decreased income limits activity;

there is the death of a spouse.

The church can assist in cultivating relationships with others and enriching lives through provision of meaningful experiences. For additional insight and help at this point, see *Senior Adult Family Life* by John C. Howell (see Bibliography).

Ongoing Church Program Opportunities

Examine the total program of your church to determine the opportunities which already exist for you to minister to senior adults. Of course, most church programs make provisions for all ages, but look for ways they minister to your older members.

Begin with corporate worship opportunities. Approximately one-fifth of the average congregation is senior adults. They should be included in plans for worship services. Visibility of senior adults in the worship services as choir members, ushers, greeters, and leaders in testimony and prayer affirms the worth of older persons in the church. Sermon topics should speak to their needs and concerns—for example, what the Bible says about aging and the old, evangelism and late life, lifelong spiritual growth, theology of personhood, attitudes toward the elderly and aging, death and dying, value of being *vs.* doing. The pastor will become aware of many other subjects as he relates more closely with this age group. An excellent treatment of the biblical teachings on aging is Frank Stagg's paper, *Biblical Perspectives on Aging.* Copies may be obtained from the National Interfaith Coalition on Aging, P. O. Box 1924, Athens, Georgia 30603.

• The church also ministers to and with senior adults through its basic program organizations (Sunday School, Church Training, missions organizations, and music). In these organizations, senior adults are considered as a distinct but not a separate group. The needs to be met are the same as for other age groups. For example, consider program content for senior adults as you consider the distinctive needs of other age groups.

The Sunday School offers Bible study opportunities which are appealing to senior adults. The need and desire to study God's Word continues throughout life. Space, leadership, organization, and study helps should be provided as carefully for this group as for any other. Other tasks of the Sunday School are outreach (enlistment) and ministry. These are dealt with in specific terms in *Working with Senior Adults in Sunday School* by Douglas Cole (see Bibliography).

Ongoing church membership training programs have been supported through the years by the generations which are now senior adults. Fellowship and learning opportunities found there are desirable to them. The church ministers to this group by provision of subject materials, organization, space, leadership, and time scheduling. Suggestions may be found in *Developing Your Adult Training Program* by Jimmy Dunn (see Bibliography).

The music ministry is for all. Many churches have age-graded choirs, including one for senior adults. Some have special musical groups such as handbell choirs, which offer additional opportunities to older persons. Those who desire to express praise and gratitude may find fulfillment in music. A church may also discover an opportunity to increase its ministry to their older members in this program.

Senior adults may find study and service opportunities in the missionary organizations of the local church. The availability of retirees affords the church excellent possibilities for volunteer ministries. Needs of older persons are also met as they find meaningful involvement in missions.

Recreation, drama, and media (library) are all ministries of the church which senior adults may share. Some activities may be planned especially for them. They should also be encouraged to participate in others which are for other ages. These and other opportunities are dealt with in more detail in chapter 7. The point here is that effort must be exerted to make these activities available to senior adults and to involve them. Making them available is not enough, though. Senior adults must be assured that they are wanted and often even encouraged to participate.

The list of ministries already available in your church is impressive. The participation of a minority of all senior adults in these ministries and the exclusion of many by neglect of church members to adequately provide and encourage may be less impressive. To enhance the ministry to senior adults, your church should objectively study and improve its provision for this group through the established organizations and ministries.

Additional Opportunities Needed

As we consider the needs and interests of senior adults, we will begin to see the need and possibilities for additional programming—especially for weekday activity. Spiritual enrichment, learning opportunities, socialization, meaningful involvement in services to others, and needs for service are also concerns of the basic programs of the churches. The provisions of these programs will meet many of these needs and interests. We should actively encourage senior adults to participate fully in those ongoing programs of Sunday School, Church Training, missions education, music, and the pastoral ministries. Any special weekday program will be in addition to that which is provided by those basic programs.

Many studies of successful senior adults show that those active in *meaningful* social and spiritual involvement have greater life satisfaction than those who are not. Isolation and loneliness, the lot of many senior adults, can be lessened by regular weekday activities. Many of the conditions attributed to poor mental health can be improved by association with others in a caring fellowship. Independence, a quality most older persons wish to maintain, is enhanced by appropriately planned ministries of the church.

The concept of weekday programs for senior adults is not new. Community senior centers were established in some areas years ago. The first club for older persons was organized in Boston in 1870. The Weban Hodson Senior Center established in New York in 1944 was the first of its kind in the United States. The second such project was begun in 1947 in San Francisco. Numbers of senior centers and major clubs have increased rapidly since then. In 1975 The National Institute of Senior Centers compiled a directory including 4,870 programs. Another 17,060 identified programs either did not respond to the survey or did not meet weekly.

Churches have been providing special ministries to the elderly since 1830, although the majority of present programs were begun after 1971, according to a survey reported by the National Interfaith Coalition on Aging in 1976. These programs range from monthly fellowship meetings to comprehensive weekday programming, offering something every day for personal involvement and for service to others.

Barriers to Overcome

Possibly there are some barriers to a weekday program for senior adults in your church. These should be examined at the outset.

* *Lack of awareness on the part of church leaders may be your first barrier.* Some need to be made aware of the needs and potential for a senior adult ministry.

* *One barrier which may be encountered then is a lack of awareness of the needs of senior adults, what they are really like, and the potential of a senior adult ministry.* This awareness and understanding can come from consciously seeing and hearing what senior adults have to say. Church leaders must be motivated to actively support all the provisions for senior adults. You and/or others who recognize this barrier must provide that motivation.

* *Some churches or church leaders have not responded to the need for special provisions for senior adults because of concern about forming another organization in the church.* We do not, indeed, need to duplicate or add organizations to do what an existing one can do. However, when we see the need to provide a ministry which is neither being provided by, nor is a logical assignment of an existing organization, then another approach should be taken. For example, we do not need to add a weekday program to minister to homebound senior adults, for that is the responsibility of the Sunday School in most churches. We need to help strengthen that work and give it our support as a ministry of the Sunday School. However, if services beyond what the Sunday School provides through the homebound ministry are needed, such as transportation or telephone reassurance, then there could be the provision of a special weekday ministry.

* *Another possible barrier is the reluctance of some to isolate and identify the elderly as a group.* Some senior adults themselves may

well raise this objection. This kind of objection is an evidence of existing stereotypes and myths which picture old age as unattractive and unacceptable. Some senior adults fail to realize the real value in peer relationships—a natural association—for all ages. In fact, there may be more value in peer relationships in the later years than in the earlier years. Support, assurance, and affirmation will more naturally come from those who have had similar experiences and are in similar circumstances. Special provisions for senior adults serve also to give recognition to the elderly, who often are neglected or ignored in groups of mixed ages.

• *"We just don't have the money to begin any new programs" is a reason some churches use for not beginning a special program for senior adults.* These churches may need to reorder their priorities or perhaps become aware of the number and needs of its older members. At least, there will be the need to recognize that responsibility for the elderly is as great as for any other age group.

• *Lack of available time by the pastor and/or staff is a valid reason for some churches not having special activities for senior adults.* Many busy pastors have made the time to start and build successful senior adult programs. These pastors have discovered that once their senior adult programs are started, they find the time to have more contact with their senior adults.

A program as outlined in the following chapter is designed to be self-sustaining—run by senior adults themselves. Remember, they are adults, capable of self-determination and operating their own programs. Staff contact is desired and needed to provide coordination and to show interest and concern. This participation is not time-consuming unless the pastor or staff insists on actively directing the program.

• *A couple of churches with which I have had contact indicate that their senior adults do not want a special program.* Perhaps there are a few churches where that is true. However, I'm inclined to believe those churches listened to only a few senior adults, probably those whose needs and interests are quite adequately met through their many activities.

This situation demonstrates the danger of calling together a small, really unrepresentative group to discuss the possibility of special activities. Later we will consider a plan to determine the needs and interests of all your senior adults. Don't be stymied by the barrier of disinterest on the part of some.

• *Some churches may find physical barriers to serving senior adults in the church facilities.* Barriers may exist in the form of foreboding stairs where ramps or an elevator are needed. Floor surfaces may be too slippery or too plush for the safety of some who walk with more difficulty. Lighting and heating/ cooling may not be adequate. Handrails may be needed at stairways, in rest rooms, and in other places. These building needs are not formidable, however, and could be corrected. No special buildings are required, although some churches do have activities buildings or youth centers which are adaptable for use by senior adults. A few churches have senior adult buildings or specially prepared space in other buildings.

Summary

The church does indeed have the resources—purpose, leadership, programs, schedule, facilities, and money—to provide an effective ministry to and with senior adults. Opportunity and potential are there. The remainder of this book will deal with how to develop and maintain such a ministry.

This study will help you begin a program or enlarge and improve the one you have. The plans are simple, but they do require work. Success in application of these principles can be an exciting adventure for you, as it has for many others who have followed similar plans to enriching experiences with their senior adults.

PART II
Planning for Ministry

3
To Prepare: Develop a Strategy

Importance of Planning

Planning is primary to developing and maintaining a senior adult ministry in your church. "Planning precedes progress" is a statement which has become trite with use, but the principle remains true.

Many criticize those who speak of planning: "We're tired of hearing about planning. Let's get on to doing something!" Considering how much needs to be done in ministry with and to senior adults, we can well understand their impatience. But what should we do? What is most needful? How can we best get it done? Who will do it? When should we do it? How will we know if we have achieved anything? The answers to these questions constitute a *plan*. Discovering those answers in a logical manner is *planning*.

- *Planning is a process through which those involved gain additional knowledge and insights*; therefore, they usually become more concerned and committed to the resultant plan.

- *Planning provides for action instead of reaction*. Without a plan one can only react to circumstances or problems as they arise. Sadly, this is often our mode of operation. We merely put bandages on untreated wounds because we have not determined how to treat them.

For example, a church may be embarrassed at not providing more

37

for its large number of senior adults. As a bandage, a senior adult activity similar to one conducted in another church is started. This reaction to an immediate concern takes no regard for the needs of their senior adults. It also does not allow for the involvement of the senior adults or the rest of the church in the beginning of a program.

Another example of reaction *vs.* a plan is having to rush to make arrangements for protective services — such as a daily contact — for an older member who, on the death of a spouse, is fearful of living alone. A telephone reassurance plan and/or a friendly visitor's plan would have the service readily available in such circumstances.

• *Planning helps detect and focus on critical needs.* Of course, we could list many of the needs of senior adults without any planning process. But planning helps to distinguish the unique needs, the more specific needs, the most critical needs, and the needs which may be best met by a church ministry.

• *Planning reduces duplication and provides for a comprehensive church program for senior adults.* It identifies gaps in ministry which need to be filled by expanding existing programs or adding programs.

• *Planning identifies resources needed and assists in obtaining them.* Too many times projects have been started and abandoned because necessary resources were not anticipated. Only limited financial or physical resources will be needed for a basic ministry to and with senior adults, but those do need to be identified.

• *Planning generates understanding and cooperation and assists in coordination.* In developing a senior adult ministry as outlined in this book, it is extremely important that it is closely coordinated with, does not conflict with, and is supportive of the basic programs of the church. The program described later involves all of the organizations of the church in their existing frameworks and suggests a plan for coordination.

• *Planning makes possible decentralization and delegation.* A plan provides a structure of activities, tasks, and responsibilities showing relationship to each other and the sequence in which they need to be done. This process allows tasks to be delegated, separates one project from another, and frees the pastor or other leaders from the responsibility of endless detail.

• *Finally, planning provides a rationale for decision making and a basis for evaluation.* Church leaders must have plans in order to properly organize, staff, direct, and evaluate programs. Effective planning should result in good plans. Through the decision-making process, objectives will be determined by which the implemented plans may be evaluated. Planning is a tool which the successful leader must use.

While planning does not guarantee success, it does increase the chances that success will occur. Lack of planning in a church promotes a kind of competitiveness that drains resources without providing the level and quality of ministry needed by all groups. For example, competing organizations may go after the same persons for leadership positions. A plan for staffing all the organizations will seek good leaders for each group. Duplicate provision of recreation activities by the church recreation program and by another group would be another example. A comprehensive plan for such provision would clarify responsibility and eliminate duplication.

On the other hand, nonplanning is a good assurance of eventual program disappearance, failure, or ineffectiveness. The church cannot afford to fail in its planning for ministry with senior adults. Remember, you are planning not only for the present but pioneering programs for the long-range future.

A Plan for Planning

Steps in planning for a senior adult ministry in a church are shown in the chart, "Developing a Ministry with Senior Adults" (next page). You will see two divisions of the steps in the first vertical column—*motivation* and *action*.

In the first two chapters, we dealt with the *motivation* steps without identifying them as such. These will not be dealt with in detail in the discussion of the planning process. However, it is extremely important that both church leaders and members be aware of the total presence and potential of the senior adults in the church. An understanding of any group is needed in order to work comfortably and effectively with them. Notice that concern comes from observation—really seeing what is going on and actually hearing what is being said.

DEVELOPING A MINISTRY WITH SENIOR ADULTS

	WHAT	WHO	HOW

MOTIVATION	Awareness
	Understanding
	Concern
		Pastor, Church Staff
		Church Leadership
			Study
			  Biblical Teaching
			  Pertinent Books
			  Observe-See, Hear

	Commitment		Church Vote Elect Senior Adult Coordinator
	Discover Needs, Interests, and Resources	Senior Adult Task Force (Senior Adult Coordi- nator and representatives	Survey Inventory
	Establish Direction	from Church Staff; Deacons; Youth;	Analyze Survey Results

	Organize	Senior Adults; and the
		basic programs of Bible
		teaching, church member
		training; missions educa-
		tion, music, and pastoral
		ministries.
			Appoint Temporary
			  Officers
			Call Meeting of Senior
			  Adults
			Form a Senior Adult
			  Council

ACTION	Plan a Balanced
	Ministry
		Senior Adult Coordinator
		Senior Adult Council
		Officers of Club
			Address 6 Areas of
			  Concern
			Consider Total Age
			  Range and Activity
			  Levels

	Evaluate and Expand		Add Components Reach Others

Commitment may appear to some to be action rather than motivation, but in this cycle I feel it more appropriately fits under motivation. As the church becomes aware, understands, and is concerned, it begins to move ideally as a corporate body. By congregational vote, the church places itself squarely behind the concept of a senior adult ministry.

The second major horizontal division of the chart is *action*. The steps listed in the *what* column are the topics of the remaining chapters.

Columns headed *who* and *how* complete a brief overview of the entire process of developing a ministry with senior adults in your church. This chart is recommended as a planning guide.

Schedule for Planning

An expanded step-by-step procedure for planning and implementing the development process will be helpful. A suggested schedule is provided in the Appendix, "A Schedule for Developing a Senior Adult Ministry" (chart). You may wish to reproduce this form or your own version of it on a large chart for use as a guide. You may put your actual dates in the *Time Frame* column. Note that the schedule suggests a senior adult emphasis month. The activities of the month provide for the motivation procedures of planning. Through this emphasis the church will be prepared for a ministry with senior adults. In addition, the attention, interest, and participation of senior adults themselves will be heightened.

Role of Pastor

The pastor should be the motivator, enabler, and facilitator for this planning project. Because it will be a churchwide effort, the pastor should lead the church to act officially to engage in the project. He should request funds for necessary supplies and ask church clerical and record-keeping personnel, whether paid or volunteer, to cooperate. He should see that the project organization is completed and then continue his personal support.

Organization for Planning

The organization for the project should be only as complex as is needed. It will consist of a coordinator, a task force, and those who will conduct the survey.

The permanent organization discussed in chapter 6 calls for a *senior adult coordinator* to be elected by the church. It would be expedient to enlist that person at this time to coordinate the planning activities. The coordinator may be a senior adult or a younger adult. The primary consideration is to obtain the services of the person in the church who loves and respects senior adults, sees their needs, wants to help them, and is willing to learn.

The task force will plan the special emphasis month, plan and conduct the survey, determine community resources for senior adults, analyze the survey, and recommend objectives and program activity components (such as a hobby group, a study group). The term *task force* is used because this body will terminate when its tasks are completed. The task force should be representative of the total life of the church. (The regular church council could function as a task force, but a special short-term group with this single responsibility would be better.)

The number of members on the task force will vary with the size of the church. The major concern is that it be truly representative. Include the pastor and/or another appropriate staff person, a young person, a deacon, a professional person in the field of aging if available, and representatives from the church's basic programs of Bible teaching, membership training, missions education, and music. Include also representatives of active and inactive senior adults. (Inactive members may need the special ministry of the church more than those who are active in everything.) The organizational representatives should be in a position to lead those organizations to be more responsive to the needs of the elderly, as may be suggested by the survey. They may also be responsible for senior adult emphasis in their programs during the special emphasis month.

The pastor or an appropriate committee of the church should be responsible for forming the task force. The senior adult coordinator will be the chairman. His first responsibility will be to lead the task force in an orientation to their work. The orientation should include an understanding of who senior adults are, what they are like, and the opportunities and responsibilities of the church for senior adults.

Then a study of the actions outlined in the suggested schedule for developing a senior adult ministry will provide an overview of what they will be doing.

Senior Adult Emphasis Month

The first action of the task force will be to determine a date for the senior adult emphasis if it was not already set by previous action of the church. Spring would be a good choice because it is a good church attendance time and is also the time usually chosen for community and national emphases on Older Americans. In setting the date, consideration must be given to time needed for preparation, as suggested in the schedule shown earlier.

Plans for the month should include weekly emphases focusing on senior adults. The suggested outline calls for using the first three Sundays to create awareness, understanding, and concern. (Specific suggestions appear in the Appendix.)

It has been suggested that the last Sunday in the emphasis be proclaimed Senior Adult Day in the church. (The Southern Baptist Convention has adopted the first Sunday in May as the recommended Senior Adult Day for churches. Baptist churches may wish to plan their senior adult emphasis to conclude on the first Sunday in May.)

The Senior Adult Day would be a time of recognition of senior adults. They should be used in as many ways as possible in the worship services, and all senior adult members should be encouraged to attend. (Additional suggestions appear in the Appendix.)

Discover Community Resources for Senior Adults

To determine eventually the directions of the church ministry with senior adults, the task force needs to be aware of provisions made for older persons by other institutions and agencies in the community. The task force should inventory the community resources and tabulate that information for their use in planning. The information can also be used in the future to provide referral services to older members. If there is a local or county council on aging, that information would be readily available from them. Otherwise, you may look to other social service agencies or to the Area Agency on Aging for such a list. The area agency can be located by contacting the state agency on aging through your governor's office.

If such a list is not readily available, then the task force should conduct its own inventory. Public health, welfare, employment, and mental health agencies should be contacted to determine what they provide for older persons in your community. Also contact the United Giver's Fund, Chamber of Commerce, Parks and Recreation Commissions, libraries, schools, Cooperative Extension Agencies, and other government and civic organizations for any services they may provide older persons. (A form which you may use for this resource inventory is provided in the Appendix entitled "Community Resources Inventory Form.")

Now that a rationale for a senior adult ministry has been examined, and a plan for determining a ministry has been set, we are ready to move to the first vital step in the process of developing a senior adult ministry for your church. You must discover the needs and interests of *your* senior adults.

4

To Begin: Discover the Needs and Interests of Your Senior Adults

Every successful senior adult ministry program studied has started with a survey to determine needs. Outstanding examples across the nation are the Chatsworth Adult Center of San Diego, the Shepherd's Center in Kansas City, and Project HEAD of Philadelphia. Numerous local church programs also report that they began with a survey of interests and needs. In many instances these have reported that the surveys showed needs for programs not originally conceived by the organizations.

The Shepherd's Center concept of a variety of services sponsored jointly by twenty-two churches in Kansas City came out of an original thought of providing housing for older persons in the area. A consultant employed to assist with the housing proposal suggested strongly that a survey of the community be made to determine the need. The survey results showed many other needs and interests to be more critical than housing. As a direct result of the survey, several thousand older persons in the area are having some of their needs and interests met, whereas the proposed housing project would have served relatively few.

Why is it we are so reluctant to take "another survey"? Could it be that the results of the last one — for whatever purpose it might have been taken — were never used? Well, you will need this one; and you will need to make use of the results. How else can you minister effectively to the senior adults in *your* church? Remember, senior adults are not all alike; they will choose to do what they want to do with their time. So you need to know what your senior adults want.

Perhaps you are thinking, too, of all those loyal older members who will attend whatever you plan; but be reminded that they are a small minority of your total potential.

I make no apology for the details suggested in preparing for, taking, and tabulating the results of this survey. Of course you can do less, starting with a smaller group; but ultimately every senior adult's needs and interests must be considered. I challenge you to make this a priority in your church. Give it the importance of a Sunday School enlargement or stewardship campaign. You are attempting to bring about a balance in your church program, focusing on what is likely 20 percent of your membership.

A Survey of Your Senior Adults

Conduct the survey during the last week of the special emphasis month. The goal of the survey is to obtain information from every senior adult in your church and Sunday School membership.

In your own experience, you have probably learned that mail surveys produce poor results. Telephone surveys are better but not very personal or productive. If you could get all the senior adults together, you could take the survey in unison. But even with the best percentage of attendance in the Sunday School being in the older departments or classes, those members are most likely still a minority of your senior adult membership. So I suggest that the survey be taken by a personal contact with each senior adult.

Who are *your* senior adults? They will be found on your church roll and Sunday School roll. Include Sunday School members who are not members of your church. You will likely be surprised to discover how many senior adults there are unless you have checked recently.

Planning for the Survey

The senior adult coordinator should obtain a list of all senior adults and have the church clerical staff or volunteers enter names, addresses, telephone numbers, and year of birth on survey cards. A sample card appears in the Appendix, "Senior Adult Needs and Interests Survey."

This form is available in quantity from Baptist Book Stores. It is on heavy card stock and punched for use in a key-sort system. You may, of course, develop your own instrument. Be careful not to promise anything you cannot deliver—don't list an activity to be chosen which you cannot possibly provide.

Write names, addresses, birth dates, and phone numbers on individual cards. Then combine cards into groups of five home addresses and place in envelopes numbered consecutively. Compile a working list and mark it accordingly as a control. Combine ten envelopes into one larger envelope, indicating the group numbers on the outside.

Enlist and Train Interviewers

Enlist an interviewer for each group of five addresses. If you have more than one hundred senior adults, enlist a captain for each ten interviewers. You may choose to enlist captains and instruct them to enlist ten interviewers each. Interviewers may be adults of any age. Don't overlook using senior adults. The coordinator, with the help of the task force, is responsible for enlisting, organizing, and training the interviewers.

Training interviewers is important. Schedule the training session prior to or following a regular service of the church. Commit all interviewers to attending the training session. The suggested outline for senior adult emphasis month has the training session scheduled for the second Sunday. A suggested list of instructions for interviewers appears here and in the packages of forms. This information may be reproduced or adapted to distribute during the instruction period.

Interviewers should understand the form and how it will be used. Demonstrate the key-sort system with a stack of previously prepared cards. Explain the information requested, and answer any question about any specific point. Remind the interviewers that they are contacting adults who can express for themselves their own interests and needs—and should be encouraged to do so. Their approach should be an attitude of helpfulness—not prompting, condescending, or patronizing.

HOW TO USE SENIOR ADULT SURVEY FORMS

Taking the Survey

Complete information on center front from church and Sunday School rolls. Blanks will be filled in by the interviewer.

Interviewer checks items in the six sections as the senior adult is interviewed. There is also space on the front of the card to record any verbal comments which should be passed on to the church. Include information such as divorced, separated.

General Information

1. Age last birthday. Check the appropriate space by referring to the date of birth if that information is on the card. Otherwise, ask for it.

2. Self-explanatory

3. Check if attend with any degree of regularity

Spiritual Enrichment

This is an "Interests" area.

Ask the senior adult if he would be interested in any additional spiritual enrichment activities. Suggest those listed as possibilities and check any of interest. Ask for other suggestions and write on the card.

Learning Opportunities

This is the second "Interests" area.

Suggest that the senior adult might be interested in special learning opportunities. Read the examples listed and check any in which there is interest. Ask for other suggestions and write on the card.

Socialization

This is the third "Interests" area.

State that the church has always played a vital part in the social lives of persons and should throughout one's life. Suggest that your church has a vital interest in the social life of senior adults and read the examples of possible activities. Check those in which interest is shown.

Service Opportunities

This is also primarily an "Interests" area.

Indicate the desire of the church in providing meaningful service opportunities for those who are interested and have the time to give. State that though one may be retired from his major vocation, he can still be useful. Read the possible service activities listed and check those in which there is indicated interest.

Services Needed

This is the "needs" area. The interviewer should use his own observation of apparent circumstance to assess needs and write on the front of the card any special reports.

Diplomatically, but positively, express the concern of the church for any member who has unmet needs. Explain that the church may not be in a position to meet all needs but that attempts are being made to discover community resources to which persons may be referred to have certain needs met; and the church is interested in responding to those needs which it can meet. Ask the senior adult to tell you how the church can help. Ask if there is need for any of the services listed. Check those so indicated. Write in any other service needs expressed.

Tabulating Results of the Church Survey

Following the survey, the information from the card may easily be tabulated. If the Key-Sort card is used, notch out holes opposite checked items. Then stack the cards facing forward and upright; slip a heavy wire or ice pick through the hole opposite the information to be counted; lift up by the wire and allow the notched-out cards to fall free. These will be the persons who indicated that need or interest.

A survey card may be used as a tabulation chart. Enter by each item the number of persons whose cards have that item checked.

A tally sheet may be needed if the Key-Sort method is not used. Make a vertical list of items from the card, with space opposite for making a mark for each card on which each item is checked. Then a count of marks opposite each item should be entered.

Other Use of the Cards

Using the Key-Sort method in two or more steps provides additional information.

Examples:

Sort out all who attend Sunday School. Stack the remaining cards and sort by age groups to determine those ages for which you need to make more provision.

To discover a teacher for a hobby group, sort out all those who indicated an interest in arts, crafts, or hobbies under Service Opportunities.

Match interest in home repairs with home repairs needed by sorting out those items under Service Opportunities and Services Needed.

All your senior adults who have expressed needs can be sorted out by using the hole opposite Services Needed. Then you can sort by each service needed and/or by combination of needs, such as Transportation, and then which of those also need Shopping Assistance.

You may find a youth sports team manager by sorting out those interested in sports participation under Socialization and further sorting out any who indicate an interest in working with youth under Service Opportunities.

You will find other ways of computing data and discovering information from this system. These cards will be valuable to you for some time, so store them carefully and use them extensively.

Any of the suggested uses of the Key-Sort Card also apply to any other form used except that forms would be handled individually by hand.

Churches with computer services may adapt these suggestions to their systems for even more sophisticated information extractions.

New Church Members

Senior adults who join your church or Sunday School should be asked to fill out a survey card to be included in the file. Expressed interests and needs will help the church minister more effectively to the new members.

Make Survey Assignments

• Make assignments by giving each captain his packet of ten envelopes, containing survey cards for five home addresses each. The captains should make the assignments to their team members, writing each interviewer's name on the large envelope opposite the group number assigned to him.

• Ask the interviewers to contact the senior adults assigned, arrange for and conduct the interviews, and return the results to the church within a week.

• Returned envelopes should be put in numerical order so that captains may check their lists.

• A checkup meeting should be held at the end of the week. Captains should then call interviewers who did not return their envelopes and encourage them to complete their assignments within three days.

• The master list should be marked to indicate returned assignment packets. Set a goal to obtain 100 percent returns within ten days of the training and assignments meeting.

• Cards on senior adults not contacted may be followed up at some later date.

(A survey card should be given every new senior adult who joins your church or Sunday School.)

Tabulate Survey Results

The results of the survey should now be tabulated to determine items of concern and the number of persons indicating each expressed need or interest. If you use the key-sort survey card, have volunteers clip out the holes adjacent to each item checked on the card. Then, with a knitting needle, ice pick, or some other such device, sort the cards by information sought. Stack all the cards turned the same way. Run the wire object through the hole opposite the information sought. Lift the cards by the wire, and all of those which have indications of that need or interest will drop from the pack of cards and can then be counted. Write the count on a blank survey card to serve as a compiled report. If some other form of survey instrument is used, then the task force and/or other volunteer will need to count each card for the number of persons indicating each specific need or interest.

You now have the data, the basic information, with which you can determine what direction *your* senior adult ministry should take.

5

To Establish Direction: Determine
Appropriate Objectives
and Activity Components

Your senior adults' interests and needs should be the basis for your church's decision about what kind of program to offer. A complete survey—such as outlined in the previous chapter—is the most accurate method for discovering needs and interests.

A chart such as the one shown here could be used to give you a clear picture of your senior adults' priority needs and interests as revealed by the survey. By putting in parenthesis beside each item the number of persons indicating that need or interest, your chart will also be helpful in establishing areas of priority.

Consider Community Resources

As you examine these lists, you will see some items which are serviced by community organizations. Indications of needs and interests should be compared with the provisions of those resources previously inventoried by the task force. A chart like the one shown here may be used to readily identify agencies and the services which they provide.

Determine and State Objectives

The task force is now ready to determine the direction your senior adult ministry should take. Suggested objectives for the church and program components for a special senior adult ministry should be determined and stated.

Based on anticipated needs and interests of many churches, I suggest the following objectives as examples only. (Remember, your directions should be determined by the specific needs and interests of your senior adults.)

PRIORITY NEEDS AND INTERESTS (Sample)

AREAS of MINISTRY

Relative Importance	Spiritual Enrichment	Learning Opportunities	Socialization	Service Opportunities	Services Needed
Highest	Bible Study (89)	Personal Enrichment (47)	Fellowship with Peers (206) / Trips (176)	Telephone (53) / Office Work (26)	Finances (41) / Health (38)
Middle	Retreats (42)	Hobbies (30)	Arts and Crafts (66)	Home Repairs (15) / Transportation (15)	Housing (27) / Visits (25)
Lowest	Counseling (7)	Academic (10)	Drama (21)	Visit (13) / Lead Others (8)	Employment (16)

(Rank according to number of indications of interest. Numbers used here are hypothetical samples for illustration only.)

COMMUNITY RESOURCES FOR THE ELDERLY   (Sample)

Community Agencies	Transportation	Health	Economic	Employment	Nutrition	Housing	Homemaker	Shopping Assistance	Other
					NEEDS				
Social Security		Medicare	✓						Referrals
Health Dept.		Nurses Shots							
American Legion		Wheel Chairs							
Council on Aging	✓				✓				Referrals
Social Service		Medicaid	S.S.I.				✓		
AARP								✓	Involvement
Housing Authority					✓	✓			
City Government	✓			✓					
Employment Service				✓					
Fire Dept.									Telephone Reassurance
Recreation Dept.									Community Social Activities

1. To give careful consideration to provisions of basic program organizations for senior adults.

2. To provide materials and activities which will enhance spiritual enrichment.

3. To offer learning opportunities for continuing growth toward self-actualization.

4. To provide attractive socialization activities to combat loneliness and to give a sense of belonging.

5. To offer opportunities for service involvement to add meaning to life and raise self-esteem.

6. To make provisions for meeting physical and safety needs as possible and appropriate.

7. To provide barrier-free facilities conducive for use by senior adults.

8. To determine community resources available to help meet needs and interests of older persons and to assist older members in obtaining that help as required.

Objective number 1 relates to the discussion in chapter 2 which indicated that the church already has ongoing programs which minister to persons of all ages. The task force must recognize the purposes and potential of those organizations to meet some of the expressed needs and interests. The accompanying chart may be helpful in determining such responsibility.

You will note that the chart speaks to the six basic programs recognized in Southern Baptist churches. Other denominations will probably have similar provisions. Note also the last column which is labeled "Special." Indications should be made in this column when task force members feel there is need for additional provision in meeting each of the needs and interests, or that particular needs and interests will not be a major responsibility or opportunity for a regular basic program.

Pastoral ministries are provided by the pastor, staff, deacons, and, in some churches, special committees. Counseling, visits, spiritual enrichment, evangelism, and worship provided must serve the needs of older persons as well as younger persons.

The Sunday School is the Bible teaching program of your church. As such, it should be responsive to the Bible study needs and interests of senior adults. Response should take the form of appropriate and

ASSIGNMENT OF MINISTRY OPPORTUNITY
(Sample)

Needs and Interests	CHURCH ORGANIZATIONS RESPONSIBLE						
	Pas. Min.	S.S.	C.T.	Music	Bro'h'd	WMU	Special
Bible Study		✓					✓
Personal Enrichment	✓	✓	✓	✓	✓	✓	✓
Study of Religions			✓				✓
Hobbies							✓
Mission Work					✓	✓	✓
Home Repairs							✓
Music Activity				✓			
Drama							
Transportation							✓
Visits	✓	✓					✓
Telephone Assurance							✓
Travel							✓
Fellowship		✓	✓	✓	✓	✓	✓

adequate provision of classes and departments in the regular Sunday morning structure. The Sunday School should assume responsibility for the provision of Bible study classes during the week as well.

Outreach to involve persons in the Bible teaching experiences and in the total program of the church is a vital part of the work. General ministry to members is another facet of its provision. Senior adults should be active participants in these activities through the Sunday School. The senior adult class provides a caring fellowship.

The church membership training organization in many churches is providing continuing learning opportunities and will be the logical organization for meeting some of the interests and needs in this area. As with the Sunday School, your Church Training program should make appropriate and adequate provision within the structure of departments and groups for senior adults. The Church Training organization may also assume responsibility for planning such opportunities during the week. Some of the fellowship needs and other needs and interests of your senior adults are also met by this organization.

The church music ministry responds to the needs and interests of your senior adults in the areas of spiritual enrichment, socialization, and service involvement. Selection of music for worship services, assistance with music in the meetings of senior adults, encouraging senior adult involvement in regular adult choirs, the provision of a special senior adult choir, planning fun singing groups, assisting senior adults in the provision of music programs for institutionalized or shut-in persons — these are but a few examples.

Men and women's missions organizations offer your senior adults opportunities for learning about missions, for meaningful involvement in mission actions, for supporting missions, and for personal ministries. Many of the special service needs of senior adults may be met through these programs.

Your task force must be realistic in its assumptions and assignments of responsibilities to the basic programs of the church. The nature of the organizations, past experiences, attitudes, and availability of leadership, time requirements, and other pertinent items must be carefully considered.

I believe in these organizations as you do. They are the basic programs of a church. I am eager to see them responsive, as many are, to the opportunities to minister to senior adults. They are parts of the total comprehensive ministry conceived for senior adults in a church. Every effort should be given to strengthening and supporting them, and senior adults should be urged to participate in each one. However, I am also aware that to arbitrarily assign all of the expressed needs and interests to these would be something less than a comprehensive ministry. Let's build on these existing programs and supplement with other activities as needs and interests indicate.

Many churches have found a need for a special organization for senior adult activities to provide added opportunities for them. These are not competing organizations, but are actually supplementary and complementary to what is being done through ongoing programs. This special organization relates to objective numbers 2 through 6. It provides a means for utilizing the weekday time of retirees and provides more opportunity for senior adults to manage their own affairs.

Determine Activities to Be Suggested

Having analyzed the survey, determined the provisions of existing resources both in and out of the church, your task force is ready now to decide what additional components of ministry to recommend.

Report on Survey Results

If you are following the suggested schedule for developing a senior adult ministry, you have now come to Sunday 4 of the senior adult emphasis month. This Sunday should be observed as Senior Adult Day, including activities such as those suggested in the Appendix. In addition, you may choose to have your survey report and discussion meeting with senior adults at a luncheon on that day.

If your task force needs more time to complete its responsibilities as outlined, schedule a rally of senior adults one day during the week following Sunday 4. The purpose of the meeting will be to share with the senior adults a summary of the results of the survey, the studies made by the task force, and recommendations growing out of that study. The senior adults should indicate their decision on whether to have a weekday program and should give some indication of the directions they feel that the program should move.

Presiding over the meeting, the senior adult coordinator should lead the group to a decision on a future meeting, not more than 30 days later, which would inititate the special program. Temporary officers could be appointed to plan the activities of the first meeting and to preside over the organizational activities. A nominating committee may also be appointed to nominate permanent officers at the meeting.

We're now ready to consider an organizational pattern.

6

To Proceed: Organize for Effective Ministry

Organization is necessary for effective work with a group, whether senior adult or any other. Though some of us are prone to speak negatively about organizing for action and express a preference for "informal approaches," we actually think and act logically in almost all we do. Organization is the logical arrangement of actions with assigned responsibilities. Simply stated, organization is a method for getting something done.

Setting objectives and identifying the needs for certain activities were discussed in the previous chapter. To accomplish those objectives and implement those activities, you must assign responsibilities.

The first step is to develop a framework which designates persons for certain assignments and responsibilities. Keep in mind that we are seeking to achieve the objectives suggested in chapter 5.

By carefully studying these objectives, you will understand the need for coordinating the provisions for senior adults in the church's basic programs and activities to meet their expressed interests and needs. As additional activities are envisioned, you must assign responsibility for planning and conducting them.

What is the best structure for the general coordination of programs and facilities for your senior adults? In answering that question, keep these two points in mind:

1. You *do not* want to superimpose an organization over the basic programs of Bible teaching, training, missions organizations, music, and pastoral ministries.

2. You *do* want to provide for participatory management, involving all who have any responsibility or opportunity to minister with senior adults, for the purpose of providing mutual support and avoiding conflicts.

60

Perhaps the best way to meet both these desired ends is through a *senior adult council.* This senior adult council should be representative of the church staff and of senior adult units of the basic programs and other major emphases of the church. Some programs will have logical representatives such as the Sunday School senior adult Class Activities Leader. The church should determine the composition of this council just as it sets up other councils or representative committees. The council then would carry out the assigned responsibilities of the overall coordination, correlation, and general information related to the ministry of the church to senior adults.

The *senior adult coordinator* should serve as chairman of the council, coordinate and/or correlate actions, set in motion any new activities planned, and represent senior adults to the church and the community.

The relationship of the council and coordinator to the programs of the church is shown by the following grid. This illustrates a structure common to many Southern Baptist churches.

Note in the matrix that the responsibility, control, and accountability for the tasks of the church are given to the basic programs and the church staff in vertical columns. Look across the church programs for a view of provisions for senior adults as a segment of the church membership. The matrix then shows the coordinating role of the senior adult council and the coordinator. This approach in no way violates principles of organization or management. If your senior adult council and coordinator operate according to the suggestions which follow, your senior adult ministry will become a comprehensive program of all these organizations working together.

The last column on the right of the grid is labeled "Special Ministries." This terminology does not suggest a lack of prominence or importance for other tasks of the church. If the words *fellowship, ministry, personal growth, spiritual enrichment, self-actualization, assurance,* or other similar terms had been used, church concern would be obvious. Several of the basic programs are also concerned about many of these areas. Care should be taken to avoid conflict by any additional programming.

The column simply shows the relationships of any special programs for senior adults with other church programs. Such programs

CHURCH ORGANIZATION MATRIX

Age Group	Assignments of Functions of a Church							Coordination
	Bible Teaching / Sunday School	Training / Church Training	Music / Music Ministry	Missions / WMU, Brotherhood	Worship / Pastoral Ministry	Evangelism / Pastoral Ministry	Special Ministries / Senior Adult Club	Senior Adult Coordinator and Council
Senior Adults								

or organizations should be treated like existing organizations in planning, coordination, and correlation efforts. This column also allows for recognition of any special organization or special activity components set up to meet some of the discovered needs and interests of your senior adults.

This special ministries organization may take the form of a *senior adult club*. For our use *club* will be a general term for whatever you call your weekday senior adult organization. Discussion about and suggestions of names appear later in this chapter.

Now we have identified three levels of organization for your senior adult ministry. Refer to the Appendix, "Senior Adult Ministry Organization Chart" (diagram) for a visual approach to organization.

In the suggested schedule for developing your senior adult ministry, your senior adult coordinator may have been enlisted and elected by the church in the early stages. (Refer to the schedule in the Appendix and the discussion in chapter 3.)

Following the survey analysis and the determination of immediate plans, the task force should be dismissed. Make plans to express appreciation publicly for the task force, the interviewers, and the others who have worked to bring your plan to this point.

The Senior Adult Council

Now is the time to form your senior adult council. Following the suggested schedule, this action should occur immediately after the special senior adult emphasis month. Obviously, some task force members may be retained on the council. In addition to representatives of the staff, basic programs, the general membership, and the senior adult club, consider other possible representation from the services and emphasis programs of recreation, library, youth, and so forth.

The pastor or staff person with responsibility for senior adults should provide a thorough orientation to the council soon after its formation. Council members must have an accurate understanding of the senior adult years, a positive philosophy on aging, an appreciation of the church's role in ministry to senior adults, and an awareness of the needs, interests, and talents of the senior adults in your church.

Supplement the material in this book with the publications listed in the Bibliography. Your denomination probably provides training conferences and workshops locally, regionally, or nationally. Community organizations often have training programs for their workers which are open to others. Community colleges, adult education programs, and universities often offer courses in gerontology—the study of human aging. Take advantage of all such opportunities. The senior adults on your council will need this training, too.

As stated earlier, the purpose of the council is to take a broad view of the church's ministry to senior adults. The council is a general coordination, correlation, and promotion group. Unlike a church council, the senior adult council focuses only on coordinating the senior adult ministry. Council members should work off of the basis of the objectives derived from the survey. They should also stay abreast of any subsequent studies or observations, evaluations of actions taken toward reaching those objectives, general church emphases, and the potential enlargement of ministry.

Meetings of the council may be quarterly or no more than semi-annually. Representatives of the various facets of the church should report on their senior adult activities. The problems and concerns of the representatives should be discussed. The success or lack of success of special activities should be noted.

Balance in the senior adult ministry as discussed in Part II (Providing a Balanced Program) should be a guide for altering or enlarging the program. Possibilities of relating senior adult ministries to special emphases and activities of the church should be considered. Coordination of planned events and activities for senior adults should take the form of an annual calendar to avoid conflicts and duplication by the various church organizations. Correlation should result in a comprehensive ministry, promoted by each church program.

The council should inspect and evaluate the buildings and facilities of the church, seeking to make them accessible, appropriate, and safe for senior adults. Recommendations for renovation, improvements, additions of equipment, reassignment of space, change in maintenance practices, and special consideration in any planned new buildings may need to be made to appropriate church committees.

Budget will be needed for some of your senior adult activities. The council should request that a special item be placed in the church budget for that purpose. Of course, the church already provides materials, space, and services for senior adults through the regular budget. However, a special budget item does indicate church commitment to a special ministry with senior adults and provides the money needed for special weekday activities. Requests and recommendations should be made through proper channels, likely the church budget committee.

Finally, the council will seek constantly to involve all senior adults in the church programs designed for them. Outreach and motivation suggestions appear in chapter 10.

The council should report to the general church council and, according to church practice, to the congregation at least annually. This report should inform the church of the activity of the council, the various senior adult activities, and senior adults' participation in them.

The Senior Adult Coordinator

The senior adult coordinator is the key person in your organization. This person should be the one in your church who has demonstrated the most interest in the total welfare of your senior adults. Other necessary qualities will be suggested later, and a job description is in the Appendix. In some churches this may be the Activities Leader of Senior Adults in Sunday School. He will normally chair the senior adult council, working closely with each representative of a church program or activity related to senior adults. In addition, he will assist the officers of the club. He will plan, initiate, and evaluate. He will also be an advocate for senior adults individually and collectively, both in the church and with agencies and organizations in the community.

The coordinator may be a staff person who has this work as a major assignment in his job description. Staff personnel known to be senior adult coordinators for their church include: assistant pastors, ministers of education, ministers of music, ministers of youth, ministers of recreation, ministers of adults, and one Woman's Missionary Union director. Larger churches are moving toward full-time ministers of senior adults just as they have ministers for other age groups. In most churches, however, senior adult ministry is only one of many assignments of an individual staff person. Under those circumstances, a volunteer coordinator should be elected to work with that staff person.

The coordinator does not run the senior adult ministry. In a real sense, he does not even direct it. Working with the council, he coordinates the total program, the work of others. As the church's specialist in senior adult work, he should interpret their interests and needs, make suggestions, and offer assistance where needed. He has no authority over the basic programs or other organizations in the church but is the liaison person who carries out the function of coordination and mutual support. Because of the nature of the club and weekday activities, the coordinator will work more closely with that facet of the ministry, but not as a supervisor.

Qualities Needed in a Coordinator

The senior adult coordinator can be a person of any age — a senior adult, a middle-aged adult, or a young adult. Be cautious, though, in enlisting a young person. While senior adults may "just love a young person," many younger persons cannot identify with or relate to older persons because they have not had much experience personally or even vicariously with older persons.

The coordinator needs to have time as well as interest to give to this important work. Look for one who is warm and sincere. Senior adults respond to sincerity and friendliness. A highly extroverted person may not be as acceptable because he appears superficial.

Patience and perseverance are absolutely necessary qualities. The work may move slowly at first. Senior adults may be slow at times to accept what will be proposed and provided. A positive outlook and a Christian philosophy of personal worth will help the coordinator to accept each senior adult and see potential in him.

The motivation of the coordinator is important. An attitude of "I just love old people" is not enough. Typically, older adults are very responsive and expressive of their appreciation for attention. A leader who is primarily motivated by a need for attention will not be effective in developing independence and in fostering programs managed by senior adults themselves. He must like older people for who they are, recognizing them as persons of worth. His relationship with older persons should be friendly and natural. He should work with senior adults to enrich their lives through the basic programs of the church and those which they themselves develop and operate. The coordinator must not be a patronizing, dogmatic, or highly emotional person. He must be aware that he does not have all the answers or skills needed; in his strong desire to help, he will become a learner as well as a leader. The motivation of the coordinator, then, should be a genuine desire to assist senior adults to find a more meaningful life.

Qualities to Be Developed

Your coordinator must know how to work with senior adults. He should be interested in all of the church organizations, encouraging the senior adults to be actively involved in them. Patience is a necessary quality. For example, senior adults must be allowed to move more slowly in decision making, in understanding and accepting new activities and instructions, and in shifting from one activity to another.

The coordinator must develop patience also in listening to the opinions and feelings which will be given freely by many senior adults. He will need patience with the more timid, who need time and attention to become involved. His patience will be tested by the temptation to do things for them instead of encouraging the senior adults. Knowing how to encourage senior adults to participate and to grow without coddling and overly sympathizing is difficult but necessary. The coordinator will need to acquire the skill of accepting individuals with their faults and handicaps without showing displeasure or shock.

The coordinator needs to know how to handle the overexpressions of appreciation and praise he will receive. He must be careful not to stay in the limelight. He must exert sincere effort to shift responsibility and praise to the senior adults themselves.

Skills in other areas such as management, promotion, and advocacy are also highly desirable. But these are the primary qualities to be sought in a senior adult coordinator.

Training the Senior Adult Coordinator

Training for the senior adult coordinator will take many forms. He must gain an understanding of senior adults and the aging process. He will need to be familiar with a variety of projects and program ideas for meeting the expressed needs and interests of the senior adults in your church. He must also be in a position to help those who plan to proceed with their chosen projects.

This book provides basic orientation and will serve as a continuing guide. A number of other good books are available. Two series of books being published by the Sunday School Board of the Southern Baptist Convention are helpful. One is a leadership series, of which this book is one. Other leadership books are *150 Ideas for Activities with Senior Adults* by Bob Sessoms and *The Senior Adult Years: A Christian Psychology of Aging* by Carroll B. Freeman. The other series is for senior adults themselves. (See Bibliography.)

Periodicals such as *Mature Living,* published monthly by the Sunday School Board of the Southern Baptist Convention, are also beneficial for individual reading. Though not primarily a leadership magazine, this particular magazine gives suggestions for weekday activities and information on what other churches are doing. Other denominations also have publications of value for training.

Seminars, workshops, and conferences are becoming more readily available through community organizations, civic groups, and denominational agencies. State agencies on aging receive funds for training from the United States Older Americans Act. These funds are often used to provide the kind of training which is beneficial to church leaders of senior adults.

The Sunday School Board of the Southern Baptist Convention offers seminars throughout the nation and workshops at fall conferences at Glorieta, New Mexico and Ridgecrest, North Carolina Conference Centers. State Baptist conventions and some local associations also offer training opportunities, sometimes with the assistance of denominational agencies. A certificate program of training is envisioned which will be a correlation of these plans. The Home Mission Board of the Southern Baptist Convention provides training opportunities through materials in their Christian social ministries programs. Other denominations offer similar materials and training opportunities.

Colleges, universities, and seminaries offer courses in gerontology, the study of human aging. Many also provide short-term special studies of interest to those who work with senior adults.

With this availability of training, the senior adult coordinator can become well informed and effective in his work.

The Senior Adult Club

The third level of organization suggested for your senior adult ministry is a weekday program—referred to here as a club. Remember, this suggestion will have grown out of your discovery that all interests and needs of your senior adults are not being met through the basic programs and is in no way to supplant or conflict with existing programs or activities.

Such group programs for older adults have been a grass-roots development, a phenomenon of the growing interest and provision in senior adult work in local churches. In 1978 4,430 Southern Baptist churches reported some form of weekday activity for senior adults, even though no specific direction or pattern of organization had been given through the denomination.

Purpose and Value

As stated earlier, the purpose of the club is to meet senior adult needs and interests which are not the full responsibility and/or assignment of one of the church basic programs. For example, a fundamental need of senior adults—indeed, all people—is interaction with other persons. Many senior adults lack sufficient opportunities for socialization. An objective of the club is to provide that opportunity in an age-group setting where identity with the group will be easily and naturally established. Social activity and entertainment should be a vital part of all general meetings.

The structure suggested here promotes opportunities for senior adults to be involved in planning and carrying out programs for themselves. Doing so meets a need for continuing self-determination. The flexibility of the weekday organization permits variety and selectivity in programming. There is no set curriculum or plan; nor is there a traditional time frame within which to work.

Membership of the Club

Every senior adult in the church membership should be considered a member of the club unless he chooses not to be. Senior adults outside the membership of your church will also be attracted or brought by friends.

Some clubs maintain a roll of those who *join* by attending and expressing interest in being active members. The advantages of the roll and an attendance record are obvious. They provide an awareness of those who are active and those who may need to be reached. Attendance records also help identify any who have become inactive for some physical reason and, therefore, need special ministries. Another benefit is that members have a stronger identification with the program and a resulting sense of belonging.

Some feel that there are disadvantages to having a roll and attendance checks. These prefer a less formal organization free of feelings of membership obligation. Participation is encouraged by general promotion and by individuals inviting others Responsibilities for awareness of special needs are left to the basic programs, particularly the Sunday School. Any club action to minister to those in need would be initiated by those who learn of the need through their participation in other church programs. A closely coordinated total church ministry with senior adults could operate this way.

I personally prefer open membership without an identifying roll. A registration of those in attendance at each meeting could provide helpful information. I believe senior adults will more readily and frequently participate in the less structured activity.

Many who need the meaningful activity the most will be the least likely to come of their own initiative. They will be the timid and shy who have experienced little social life and fear embarrassing themselves in a group.

Others may not recognize the need in their own lives. Some will feel the need but be apathetic. Still others feel that they have failed in life and that no one would want them around. Then there are those who have experienced hurt because of the loss of loved ones, feelings of being slighted by the church and others, or feelings that life has not been good to them; so they isolate themselves.

Welcome those who come readily and constantly seek ways to involve the others. (Chapter 10 offers suggestions.)

Club Meetings and Weekday Activities

The senior adults themselves should determine the scope of weekday activities, including the club meetings. From the tabulations of the survey and subsequent analysis, the task force should have developed recommendations. These recommendations were to have been made to the first meeting of senior adults—the one scheduled for Sunday 4 of the Senior Adult Emphasis Month or one day during the following week. Acting on the recommendations, your senior adults chose the program proposal to be submitted to the church for approval.

At the beginning of your senior adult weekday program, let's assume that a regular general meeting is the minimum recommendation agreed upon. Many clubs begin with a monthly meeting with a planned program of fellowship, inspiration, information, and sometimes recreation. Others have started with weekly general meetings to fill a need for more frequent fellowship.

The general meeting will meet some of the interests and needs as shown in chapter 8. However, as you examine all the interests and needs expressed in the survey, you may decide that additional activities are needed. Each such special provision is called an *activity component*.

Examples of activity components are a Bible study group, a handcraft group, and a special ministries group. These components are part of the organizational structure discussed later in this chapter.

Several meeting schedules to accommodate the general meetings and activity component meetings are shown on the following chart.

In any of these plans a senior adult would have freedom to participate in any of the scheduled events. The advantage of Plans 2, 3, and 5 is that they provide more frequent opportunities for participation.

Many combinations and variations of these plans are possible. Ultimately your church could have something going on for senior adults almost every day of the week.

VARIATIONS OF MEETING PATTERNS

Alternatives	WEEKS of the MONTH			
	1	2	3	4
Plan 1		General Meeting Fellowship Inspiration Information		
Plan 2	General Meeting	General Meeting	General Meeting	General Meeting
Plan 3	Trips	General Meeting	Arts, Crafts, Hobbies Study Groups	Services to Others
Plan 4		Bible Study General Meeting Arts, Crafts, Hobbies		
Plan 5	Study Groups Arts, Crafts, Hobbies Drop-in Center Open Daily	General Meeting Drop-in Center Open Daily	Study Groups Arts, Crafts, Hobbies Drop-in Center Open Daily	Services to Others Drop-in Center Open Daily

The regular, general meeting of the club should be the hub of all weekday activities. Some senior adults refer to that meeting as their "club." I like the concept of all the weekday activities being a part of the club.

Club Organization

At the club level, senior adults should plan, develop, and lead their own programs. Whatever organizational structure you adopt, the leadership positions should be elected and filled by senior adults. As natural as it may seem, senior adult volunteers to lead their peers may not be spontaneous. The coordinator and other church leaders must provide encouragement. Also, assure your senior adults that you have no thought of the club leaders being mere figureheads. That assurance comes from careful avoidance of any given directions and any indication of control by the coordinator. The coordinator should be careful to refer to the survey results as the reason for any suggestions.

Self-direction is also motivated by frequent recognition of leadership positions. You may do so verbally as long as you do not flatter or appear insincere. Recognition is better expressed by insistence and persistence that the officers do the work to which they have been elected (and your not doing it for them).

The senior adult coordinator may find it far easier, and maybe even more self-fulfilling, to do the planning, make the decisions, operate the program, and lead the activities. To do so, however, is self-defeating for the senior adult ministry, especially at the club level.

You may find that the senior adults in your church are slow to accept the responsibility for their own programs. If so, you will need to challenge the group to self-action. The pastor can help do this in a message at the organizational meeting, defining the role of the coordinator as a supporter and an aid, not a program planner and activity leader. A senior adult from another church may be asked to tell about his club's successes under senior adult leadership. Be sure he is someone with whom your senior adults can identify. Never put your senior adults in a position where they may say, "Well, we could do that *if* our church was that big or wealthy—*if* we had a leader like that — *if* we were in a big city." To motivate, you must picture a highly possible as well as attractive program.

Remind the senior adults that they have been decision makers and have been managing their own affairs for a long time; now they will continue to do so in *their* club. Another encouragement to the more timid will be the information that suggested plans, programs, and activities are available — that leaders will not be left entirely to their own ingenuity to design a program and the planned activities. Assure them that opportunities for training, such as suggested for the coordinator earlier in this chapter, will be provided.

If you have strong potential leaders, you are fortunate, but there are some cautions. Some strong personalities may not wish to follow the church-elected leaders of the senior adult ministry. They may want complete autonomy without any strings attached. They can be demanding and rebellious. The coordinator's position in this case should be patient but strong insistence on adherence to a coordinated plan for a total church ministry as expressed in the objectives stated earlier and as refined and interpreted by the senior adult council. The coordinator should also insist that the wishes of all the members be considered. The senior adult club must not become the kingdom or domain of one or several, a clique, of some few strong senior adults.

On the other hand, the coordinator should seek to channel the strong leadership abilities of such persons to meet the objectives and purposes of the senior adult club. But to do so takes patience, diplomacy, and motivation by a spiritual desire to accept persons as individuals and to help them develop their full potential in Christ and in the work of his church.

Avoid the pitfalls of allowing the vocal and prestigious to assume all the leadership roles, however motivated they may be. Seek to develop others to allow them to grow in self-concept. This broad base of leadership assures more democratic, grass-roots consideration of the wishes of the entire group.

The probabilities of loss of truly representative leadership are greater as the size of your group and the complexity of the program increases. Carefully determine and state the duties and tenure of the officers and activity chairmen. Officers and the activity chairmen should serve for a year, preferably coinciding with the church calendar year. You may wish to suggest to the club that no person should serve more than one or two consecutive terms, allowing more persons to be actively involved.

Officers

Your club organization should be as simple as possible but as complex as necessary to assure effectiveness. Avoiding complexity should not preclude involving as many persons as possible. Seek a balance, keeping in mind that most senior adults will not be patient with an unwieldly bureaucracy. The organization suggested here provides for clubs of all sizes and programs of varying activities. For a diagrammed approach, see the Appendix, "Senior Adult Ministry Organization Chart."

The smallest club will need a president, a vice-president, and a secretary. Larger clubs may add committees for such functions as enlistment of members, visiting members, planning and serving refreshments, planning the program for general meetings, or decorating the meeting room. Small or large clubs can use the plan for activities which are in addition to the general club meeting. Committees, if there are any, are to assist with the general meeting only and should not be confused with activity components.

The president, vice-president, and secretary should be nominated and elected by the senior adults at the organizational meeting as shown on the schedule in the Appendix and discussed in chapter 3. The elections may be handled in any of the accepted ways. Do not allow the process of electing officers to overshadow the primary purposes of inspiration, fellowship, and information in the general meeting. At the same time, make this a meaningful experience, demonstrating the democracy of the club and the lack of dominance by the coordinator or church staff.

Activity Components

Ideally, chairmen of activity components should be selected from those who have indicated an interest in that activity. The successful program of the Shepherd's Center in Kansas City has been built by this procedure. Club officers, with the assistance of the coordinator, should seek out and enlist a leader to plan, implement, and conduct each activity suggested by the survey and agreed upon by the senior adults attending the survey report meeting.

Conceivably, a large area of responsibility such as "Service Opportunities" may need to be further divided. For example, "Service Opportunities" could include telephone reassurance, transportation, and home repairs. Each of these would require planning, enlistment, organizing, and directing, which should be the responsibility of an individual. Subchairmen enlisted for each of these activities would be in keeping with the organization's pattern, which provides the necessary controls and channels for assistance. (See chap. 9 for further information on activity components.)

Duties of Officers

The *president* is the chief officer of the club. He represents the club on the senior adult council. He serves as head of the executive committee of the club, which consists of the officers and chairmen of the activity components. He is responsible for planning with the executive committee, seeing that plans are carried out, and evaluating the total program of the club. He presides over the general meetings. He works closely with the coordinator to accomplish the objectives of the total senior adult ministry and to correlate with the other programs of the church. He may represent the club and/or senior adults on various church committees, such as the recreation committee.

The *vice-president* is the program and promotion officer. He suggests programs for general meetings to the executive committee, enlists program personalities, and prepares all the details of the general meeting program. He may have committees to assist with this function. He is also responsible for promoting attendance. He reports on the meetings through regular church channels of communication—announcements, bulletins, newsletters, and bulletin boards. He should also communicate directly with senior adults—through a senior adult newsletter, telephone committee, and announcements in other senior adult meetings and all available media resources. If a publicity committee is formed, he will be responsible for its functions. He will work closely with the president and assume any of his duties made necessary by his absence.

The *secretary* is responsible for the club membership roll and attendance records if your club decides to have them. He will serve as host for greeting senior adults as they arrive for meetings. A committee may be enlisted for greetings, or the secretary may enlist individuals to serve at the general meetings. The secretary should provide name badges for each person to wear. He should make reports of meetings to the executive committee. He will keep minutes of the executive committee meetings and the reports of the activity components. In the absence of the president and vice president, the secretary will preside over general meetings or executive committee meetings.

The *activity component chairmen* are responsible for planning, organizing, and conducting the areas of activity assigned to them. They may enlist others who are interested in those specific activities to assist them. They serve on the executive committee and thus become a part of the total planning group. These chairmen work closely with the president and the coordinator. They report to the executive committee on the activities of the components. They are not necessarily instructors of activities but are responsible for enlisting instructors according to the nature of the activities.

In enlarged organizations where subchairmen are required, the chairmen are responsible for giving them support and receiving reports on their activities.

Club officers obviously may also be active as participants in some of the club's activities. They should be cautioned that when they enter into an activity—a hobby, for example—they are there on the level of all other participants and should be careful to assume that role rather than one of leadership. In her book Creative Programming for Older Adults, *Florence Vickery points out the difficulty peer member-leaders may have in constantly changing from an objective-being leader to a subjective-viewing member and vice versa. The coordinator can be helpful at this point.*

Training of Officers

Being a senior adult does not fully equip one to work with senior adults. Understanding the aging process and the later years, accepting age philosophically as a fact of life, being aware of the differences of individuals in the age group, seeing potential improvement in the meaning of life for those in poor health or extreme old age — all these things must often be taught to senior adults. Planning techniques, leadership principles, and program ideas and how to carry them out are important to the success of the senior adult club. Club officers should be committed to learning, and the coordinator and other church leaders must be committed to providing the training needed.

Individual and group study should be encouraged. Suggestions appear in the section "Training the Senior Adult Coordinator" earlier in this chapter.

Club Names

The word *club* may seem inappropriate as applied to a group or activity in a church. Therefore, many senior adult groups have chosen names for their ministry which they use instead of *club*. Some of those names arise from terms commonly applied to this age group. Examples are the *60-Plus, Over Sixties, Golden Agers, Senior Adult Group, Senior Adult Fellowship*, and *Senior Citizens*.

Other names seem to be a play on not admitting one's age. Since the acceptance of one's age and a realization of the positive factors of that particular period in life is important to one's integrity, many choose not to use these names even though they are quite popular. Examples of this type are *Young in Heart, Young at Heart (YAH), Just Older Youth (JOY)*, and *Actkeens*.

Other names deal with age but in a more positive way. Some examples are *Golden Agers, Keen Agers, Best Agers, Jolly Elders, Second Milers, Salt Bloc, Top Agers, Extra Years of Zest (XYZ), Prime Timers, Wise Old Owls (WOO), Fossils* and *Metalic Club*.

Names also come from an attempt to express the purpose of the club. Examples of this are *Live Long and Like It (LLL), Be Active and Live Long (Ball), Merry Makers, Live Embers, Pioneers, Golden Harvesters*, and *Evergreens*.

Your group will probably come up with a name which will be appropriate for your church's senior adult ministry. You may wish to ask for suggestions, encouraging everyone to give ideas and to vote on the possibilities.

Perform the Doing of It

A man invited his friends and neighbors to his workshop to view a machine which he had built. One of his neighbors asked what the machine was for—what it could do. In reply the builder of the machine said that it was not built to do anything; it was just a well-built, smooth-running mechanism.

It would be possible for you to perfect an organization for senior adult ministry in your church which would accomplish nothing unless it is put to work to achieve the purposes for which it is perfected. *It would be better not to have made a survey and set up an organization if the necessary effort is not given to produce the desired results:* meeting the needs and the interests of your senior adults. *The survey and organization efforts hold out promise to the senior adults which you must now fill.*

Although it is difficult, maybe impossible, to provide all things for all persons, we may be challenged by Paul's statement: "I am made all things to all men, that I might by all means save some" (1 Cor. 9:22). With that attitude and motivation, you will want to provide a balanced program of weekday activities which, added to the activities of the basic church programs, will meet the needs and interests of your senior adults.

PART III
Providing a Balanced Program

A balanced program will take into account the many variables found in your senior adult group. *Program* as defined here is more than a schedule of activities. In its broadest sense, program is what we have been referring to as a total church ministry with and for senior adults. It is all that the church does for senior adults and all that the older persons themselves experience in and through the church.

In a narrower sense, *program* is defined as the activities through which senior adults will have their needs and interests met. In this context, an activity may be planned which in and of itself does not appear to make a significant contribution but does provide a setting in which needs can be met. The activity itself is not as important as what senior adults experience in that activity.

For example, a program in one church provides an unstructured activity each Thursday morning to which a number of senior adults are transported by volunteers. A brief devotional or message may be presented. Refreshments are provided. Most of the time is spent in informal, spontaneous activities, individually, in small groups, or by the total group. On the surface, those Thursday mornings may not seem a worthwhile use of time. Beneath the surface, however, you will see the need for socialization being met. Most of these senior adults live alone, scattered throughout the city because of urban development in the central city where they once lived as neighbors and friends. This setting has allowed newcomers to find a social group with which to identify. Of course, this activity is not the only one provided for senior adults in that church, but it is a vital part of their balanced program.

You've become aware of the expressed needs and interests of your senior adults from the survey. Other factors affecting a balanced program will be obvious as you consider your group. Levels of physical activity, the wide age spread, numbers of men and of women, degrees of extrovertedness-introvertedness, education levels, economic conditions, living arrangements, and involvement in other activities — all will demonstrate the need for variety to appeal to the total group. A review of chapter 2 will help you in your observation of the differences within your group.

Balance is so important to a comprehensive ministry with senior adults that a large part of this book is given to the subject. We will approach the subject from some basic considerations, then the makeup of the general meeting of the club, and finally the five major content areas which must be considered. You will find some program considerations given as examples in these three chapters. However, it is not my primary purpose to provide ideas for programs. I recommend the book *150 Ideas for Activities with Senior Adults* by Bob Sessoms as a resource for such program help (see Bibliography).

7

Observe Special Concerns

Observe Special Concerns

Before getting into more specific suggestions about your senior adult ministry, let's consider some general concerns. These concerns affect all of our programming.

Levels of Need

Soon you will begin to place your members in Maslow's hierarchy of needs chart, shown in chapter 1. While it is difficult, maybe impossible, to categorize a person totally in one of those levels, his behavior may be better understood if you understand that he is most concerned about needs at a particular level.

For example, one of your senior adults may be reluctant to become involved in a study program designed to enrich life. You discover that he has a low opinion of himself. You realize that his self-esteem needs are not being met. Or maybe he is so concerned about his physical needs that he views the activity as frivolous. We must accept the senior adult where he is and help him grow in his interests and pursuits to the highest level in Maslow's list, self-actualization. At that level, he will be reaching toward his greatest human potential and beyond that to God's standard of perfection (Matt. 5:48; Eph. 2:10).

Studying individual survey cards will be helpful in understanding your senior adults' levels of needs. In fact, the cards should be tabulated to determine the number of persons who have expressed needs in the five categories listed on the survey card. Not only will such a tabulation help your understanding; you will also be better able to balance your program offerings. Program offerings should be based on percentages expressing needs and interests in each of the general areas.

Physical Activity Level

All of your senior adults probably cannot physically do everything that you plan. Age is a determinant, but we all know some eighty-year-olds who are physically incapacitated, some who are only slightly active, and some who are very active. The same is true of sixty-year-olds. Generally, though, your older senior adults will require activities which are less physically demanding.

A chart developed by Herbert Shore, executive director of the Golden Acres Home for the Aged in Dallas, Texas, shows the relationship between activity levels and types of programs needed.

RELATIVE NEEDS BY ACTIVITY LEVEL*
Total Population Age 60 +

Go-Go 15%	
Will-Go 35%	Social Needs
Slow-Go 35%	
No-Go 10%	Physical Needs
Can't-Go (Institutional) 5%	

*Chart used by permission of Herbert Shore, Executive Director, Golden Acres Home for the Aged, Dallas, Texas.

Note that this diagram is of all senior adults, and it does not categorize them by age. Some persons of all ages are in each of the levels of activity. This chart indicates approximate percentages of senior adults who are likely to participate in the various levels of activity, as well as those who will need more services provided to them. A careful analysis of your survey results may give you more accurate percentages for your group.

From this chart as well as previous discussions, you will probably perceive that we are concerned with two elements in balanced programming: (1) organization of senior adults as a self-interest group; (2) organization to meet the needs of the elderly. Most senior adults have the physical capacity to take care of their daily requirements. The physically active need enrichment programs. The moderately impaired need some support programs. The frail or vulnerable elderly need individual programs to assist them with survival needs.

Unexpressed Needs

Doubtless, some of your senior adults will not have indicated activities they might want because their needs rise up as barriers to their participation. If a senior adult knows he has no transportation to the church, he may rationalize that he does not want to be involved in an activity. A careful study of services needed may help you understand the lack of expressed interest in some areas.

At this point, you need to determine what unexpressed needs and interests a balanced program should address. Some suggestions may appear on the survey cards in the space provided for remarks. Suggestions may also be obtained by those who provide outreach and services to those with needs.

Some may have indicated no needs or interests. Possibly, some already have their interests and needs met. They will be needed in your program to provide leadership and support to others. Through such service even the most self-sufficient will experience growth and greater meaning in life. A balanced program will provide challenge for these.

Special Needs of Men

You will find that many activities which appeal to women will not appeal to men. Women have probably been more involved in social, study, and service activities than men. They will, therefore, respond more readily to the types of activities commonly provided for senior adults. Special care must be given to provisions which will attract and involve men.

Remember, the associations and activities of men have more often been related to their work. Their leisure was probably centered in the out-of-doors: team sports, fishing, hunting, golf, home maintenance, and other skills pursuits. Their conversations have centered on current events, politics, sports, and their work.

To meet their needs — which may have not been expressed on the survey cards — activities must be provided which capitalize on previous interests and provide an outlet for idle skills. These activities will vary by geographic location and the major occupations of the area. For example, in a seacoast town which has a major fishing industry, woodworking probably would not appeal immediately to the retired men. Making or repairing nets might.

An informal coffee club where men could meet and talk might be a better beginning. Providing help for widows of their friends and for other retirees who cannot do everything for themselves would be a higher motivation. As you observe the men in your senior adult membership, suggest ideas to the men as possible activities.

Location of Activities

Another element in a balanced program is location. While most activities will naturally be at the church, also consider opportunities for senior adults to experience activities outside the church. Many service opportunities will be in the community where senior adults go out to minister to others or to do volunteer work in other programs. Cooperate with community programs for senior adults to prevent group isolation of your senior adults and to take advantage of activities in which your group may be interested.

For example, a group of churches in your area may have an organized program of quarterly meetings. A community center may have a special program at which your group will be welcome. Trips to places of interest and special benefit — one-day or overnight — are attractive to many senior adults. A church retreat or participation in a retreat or conference planned by your denomination is a valuable contribution to a balanced program.

Frequency of Activities

Frequency as well as types of meetings at the church affect balance. A monthly meeting allows for meeting some needs. However, a balanced program that considers the various facets of ministry to senior adults themselves can hardly be achieved by one meeting per month. The alternate plans of meetings suggested in chapter 6 allow for special interest groups (activities components) to meet at other times during the month, thus providing better balance.

In your church program for senior adults, some content areas are the responsibilities of basic programs. For example, Sunday School may have total responsibility for the spiritual enrichment of all senior adults; Church Training may have the responsibility for continuing education for all senior adults; the missions programs may have total responsibility for ministry and service opportunities for and to all senior adults. If this is true of your church, your senior adult club will have major responsibility only in the area of socialization, which need could be met to a degree in monthly meetings. Even in this hypothetical case, however, notice that the frequency of activities for senior adults is more than monthly, for most basic programs meet weekly.

A balanced program requires that you give frequent opportunities for senior adults to participate. Because a program operated by senior adults themselves is advocated and because a minimum amount of time for other church leaders is required, begin to think in terms of an activity each week in order to present a balanced program.

8

The Regular General Meeting

Because the general meeting will probably be monthly—or at the
most weekly—and because it needs to consider the varied interests of
your senior adults, you should be concerned with a balance of activities in those meetings. As stated earlier, the purpose of the general
meetings is to provide fellowship, inspiration, and information.
Activities should begin with the earliest arrival and continue until the
last departure.

Pre-Session

Fellowship is enhanced by a warm greeting to each person as he
arrives. The club secretary is responsible for this. He may do it himself or enlist others to serve in this capacity.

Some activity related to preparation for the program could be
assigned to those who come early. Personal interest and careful intro-
ductions should be given newer members and the more timid. Materials laid out on a table, automatic slide presentations, recorded
music, or table games allow for immediate participation by early
arrivers.

Inspiration

Vary the *inspirational* part of your meeting from time to time to
maintain interest. Some will like a typical devotional message; others
will prefer poetry; still others will choose inspirational music. Audio-
visual materials may also be used for variety. For devotional messages
use senior adults themselves more frequently than outsiders. The pastor and other staff members should speak only occasionally.

Information

The *information* features should be balanced between things senior adults need to know and subjects of general interest. Subjects can range from Social Security benefits to a new community center for performing arts or the effects of a proposed bond issue. Don't overlook featuring senior adults who have interesting stories to tell about themselves, trips they have taken, or other activities in which they are engaged. One club features a member at each meeting, learning about his former home, former work, family, hobbies, and other interesting facts.

Entertainment

Entertainment may also be a feature of your general meeting. The talents of your own members as well as outside guests should be used. Also use group activity entertainment to encourage participation.

Post-Session

If some linger after the meeting, waiting for transportation or just because they do not want to leave, encourage their involvement in the kinds of things you arranged for the early arrivals. You may not have this problem if the facility must be closed upon dismissal.

Insofar as possible, provide something for the senior adults to do during all the time they are at the church for the general meeting.

9

Offer Balanced Content

Offer Balanced Content

A successful senior adult ministry must provide a balance in content. Realizing the variety of senior adults and the need to provide for all, think now of the five content areas of ministry with senior adults: spiritual enrichment, learning opportunities, socialization, service opportunities, and services needed. Of course, the basic programs and activities of the church will already be providing many of these ministries. But correlation by the coordinator and the council should avoid conflicts or duplications between these and the club organization. You have discovered, though, the need to provide additional opportunities in all of these content areas during the week through the club framework.

SPIRITUAL ENRICHMENT

The senior adult years provide great potential for persons to grow spiritually. The pressures of time and responsibility are lessened. The experiences of life give deeper meaning to the teachings of the Bible. Many senior adults have increased interest, and all have the need. The tabulation of your survey will show how much your members participate in the regular activities provided for spiritual enrichment. You may find your church needs to seriously consider its responsibility in helping senior adults grow spiritually. Check the section of the survey card labeled "Spiritual Enrichment" to see what additional spiritual enrichment opportunities your senior adults want.

General Provisions

In your worship services, the needs and interests of senior adults should be considered. Sermon topics and applications, music selection and presentation, prayers and prayer leadership—in fact, every facet of the service should reflect concern for senior adults as well as other age groups. The Bible study and application of its teachings in senior adult classes should be of the highest quality. The senior adult's relationship with God can be strengthened partly by increased knowledge, but more by relating teaching to experiences and concerns.

The other spiritual emphasis weeks throughout the church year must also be planned with senior adults in mind. Many churches have evangelistic and spiritual revival weeks which may ignore the needs of older persons. Not all senior adults are Christians, so they need the experience of Christian conversion and being rightly related to God. Some senior adults are spiritually inactive and need to be reenlisted and revived. Others need the growth experience of helping others during these emphasis weeks.

Other kinds of emphases such as stewardship and Bible study also provide for spiritual growth and development. Do not neglect senior adults in these plans. Give special consideration to the time of day, probable weather conditions, and content as you relate these programs to your older members. Daytime activities, transportation, recognition in the services, opportunity to meet the guest leader, and other special plans will enhance the senior adults' opportunity to benefit from special emphases.

Senior adults should be meaningfully involved in service through the basic programs as a means of spiritual growth. Through the Sunday School, for example, they can be effective witnesses and visitors in outreach to the unenlisted.

Group studies of subjects such as prayer, worship, Christian ethics, philosophy of religion, Christian ministry, missions, and participation in church music add to their spiritual growth.

Special Provisions

In cooperation with the opportunities provided through the basic program activities, certain weekday activities may be the responsibility of the senior adult club.

For example, formal and informal spiritual enrichment study groups may interest your senior adults. These groups could be ongoing activities or short-term projects. The formal group would have a teacher/lecturer who would be responsible for the structure of the study. In the informal setting the leader would guide the discussion. To keep the informal group from being an exercise in sharing present knowledge, use a resource book or books, a film, or a resource person. The subjects could include prayer, salvation, assurance, death and dying, philosophy of religion, Christian ethics.

In some churches prayer/spiritual enrichment groups have been formed by individuals who have felt such a need. These groups meet informally at a regular time each week to share personal experiences; to discuss personal, church, and community concerns; and to join in prayer related to the discussions.

Retreats and conferences offer additional opportunities for spiritual enrichment. Your club may plan such an event or join an association of churches or a denominational activity. These concentrations of time in select environments with close associations with other persons often give senior adults impetus for more rapid spiritual development. Examples of a senior adult retreat program and a conference agenda are included in the Appendix.

Resources

Materials for individual spiritual growth as well as resources for group activities should be provided through the church media center (library). Cassette tapes and books may be easily obtained and distributed. Availability of the materials will, of course, not assure their use. Inform the senior adults of their availability and encourage their use. Senior adults respond readily to large-print books and cassette players for loan.

Perhaps the simplicity of these suggestions causes you to wonder when to look for something more innovative. Remember that these suggestions have proven beneficial to the lives of many. You probably have heard of senior adults who have found in such Christian opportunities the assurance they needed to face adversity.

Summary

In a balanced ministry for senior adults, don't overlook opportunities for spiritual enrichment. The whole church is responsible. The

club can plan those activities which are not done by the other programs of the church. These may take the form of regular groups,
annual events, testimonies, special displays at meetings, and personal
encouragement to any who may have special needs.

LEARNING OPPORTUNITIES

General Provisions

A balanced program of senior adult ministry will provide attractive learning opportunities. Obviously there will be some overlapping
of content areas. We have already considered learning opportunities
which are related to spiritual enrichment. Learning will also be a
part of some of the socialization and service involvement activities.

Your church probably provides Bible study for all ages on Sunday
mornings and at certain special emphases during the year. If your
church has a Sunday evening training or study program, it probably
offers studies in doctrine, personal growth and development, church
history, and Christian ethics. Missions or organizations for men and
women provide regular and special studies in missions, world religions, and customs in other countries. The church may also provide
a special study during the year on the family or a Christian home
emphasis. Some churches have a Vacation Bible School for senior
adults each year. Special weeks may also be provided for topics
already listed as probabilities for the Sunday evening training hour.
(See the Bibliography at the end of the book.)

Many senior adults are ready to go beyond the ongoing and special
opportunities offered by their church and to be engaged in other
study programs. Possibilities of areas of interest and structures for
study are almost unlimited.

Informal Groups

The experiences of most churches and senior centers (community
centers for senior adults) reveal that senior adults respond more
readily to informal learning opportunities. This fact is true perhaps
because senior adults have not been in a formal education structure
in a long time; they may have received little formal education; they
are more subject to embarrassment where evidence of learning is

required; and they lack motivation to learn a body of knowledge for which there is no apparent use. Even in informal groups some will be reluctant to express themselves. Passive participation may actually meet the need of that type of person. Never pressure a senior adult to participate actively.

Forms and subject matter of informal groups are varied. Each group needs a leader enlisted from those who have expressed an interest in this activity. If there is only one such learning activity, this person may be the chairman of that activity component. If you have several learning groups, the chairman will be responsible for organizing and enlisting leaders for each group. Beyond the leader, the group may structure itself as it chooses or as the situation demands. For example, if refreshments are served, a person or committee may be assigned that responsibility.

A discussion group may use books, motion pictures, or audio or videotapes as resources. The range of subjects could include understanding the senior adult years, spiritual and personal enrichment, nutrition, world affairs, budgeting, finances, politics, legal matters, home safety, world religions, current events, history, defensive driving, and care of one's car.

Another kind of informal learning group is one which is participatory. This group might need an instructor in addition to a leader, depending upon the knowledge and skills of the participants. These groups could get into such things as gardening, learning new crafts, expanding hobbies, developing manual skills, financial investments, home repairs, physical fitness, creative writing, oral history, or advocacy.

Still another kind of informal group might be one which learns from observation. This group would make field trips to see places, persons, and things of interest, and see travelogues presented by lecturers and/or films. Films are available from a number of sources which are listed at your local library.

Formal Groups

Formal learning opportunities may also be needed in your balanced program. In this instance, the study group would probably have a teacher to give direction to the group. This person would not necessarily be a lecturer, even though some senior adults will be more comfortable in a lecture-receiving environment than in one in which they are expected to join in a discussion. Further structuring of the group will depend on its nature and members. If the group is engaged in a study for credit, a monitor may be needed to keep the roll and make required applications. If this is a continuing group which will be choosing a variety of subjects, and therefore needing different teachers, assign a leader to sustain that fellowship and continuity. If this group is the only unit in the club organization providing learning opportunities, then the leader should be designated as the chairman of that component in the club organization. If there are other learning groups, then this leader should work closely with the chairman of the activity component.

A formal group may also study books on the developmental needs of senior adults or any other appropriate subjects. More technical studies are possible here, perhaps, than in the informal group. For example, academic subjects such as languages are possibilities.

A variation of the formal group would be an adult education, college, or university program. Some of your senior adults might attend such an activity as a group, being identified as such a unit in your club organization; or you may arrange for those classes to be taught in your church for senior adults in your community. You may find such a program especially designed and funded for senior adults through a local college or university system.

Summary

As you balance your program by providing learning opportunities, check again to see what your survey revealed as being of interest to your senior adults. You may want to invite everyone who has indicated an interest in any kind of study opportunity to form a group and begin with a study on which they will all agree.

As you begin your first group, keep these principles in mind:
- Try for an informal, relaxed approach.
- Have one person definitely in charge.
- Make sure there is an agreed-upon definite subject.

• Provide the technical assistance needed through an instructor and/or curriculum materials, depending upon the nature of the study.

• Inform all your senior adults of the opportunity, especially those who have indicated an interest in such an activity.

SOCIALIZATION

General Provisions

Socialization is the area most of us think of first when we think about a senior adult ministry. Indeed, the need for interaction with others continues throughout one's life.

In a balanced program of socialization for senior adults, your church should look to its ongoing and special activities provided for all members and to its senior adult club organization. Regular and special meetings of the church organizations and of the congregation for worship provide opportunity for interaction with others. Recreation, including Sunday night fellowships, sports, banquets and luncheons, celebrations, camps, picnics, and other such activities enhance the opportunities for socialization in the church.

The senior adult coordinator should confirm that the church includes senior adults in all such plans. Unless they are kept in mind, activities can be planned in such a way that it will be difficult for senior adults to participate. Time, place, cost, and program agendas are factors. Consideration of senior adults might, for example, lead a church to plan some Sunday afternoon church fellowships rather than having all such affairs at night.

Senior adult Sunday School classes and other groups will probably provide social opportunities outside of the regular meeting time. Any plans made by the club will need to correlate with those events. Your senior adult council should be the clearing house for all such plans.

The Club Meetings

One of the major purposes of the club's general meeting is fellowship. As stated earlier, the time before the meeting actually starts provides a time for informal socialization. That time may be enhanced by the availability of table games, an informal seating area for conversation, music, some planned activities for individuals or small groups whhich relate to the program of the day, and/or by having hosts/hostesses assigned to stimulate social interaction as senior adults arrive. You can build fellowship in the general meeting by recognition of birthdays, anniversaries, and other individual special happenings. A meal or refreshment time provides for fellowship. You may wish to have a mixer-type game or activity occasionally so that individuals don't isolate themselves with the same person or small group all the time.

Officers of the club should be constantly alert to those who may need encouragement to interact with others and to join in the activities. Note this word of caution: Don't try to force persons to enter into an activity in which they would prefer not to be involved.

A group spirit and identity for each person should be an objective of the club general meeting. Your club might also arrange to visit and meet with a club in another church to enlarge the socialization opportunity.

Special Provisions

Beyond the general meeting, other socialization opportunities should be provided either on the same day as the general meeting or at other times during the month as suggested in chapter 6. These activities should be planned according to the interests expressed in the survey. As indicated in our discussion of learning opportunities, you may need to encourage combinations of interests and needs in order to have sufficient numbers for an activity group. Each activity group will need a designated leader who will be responsible for obtaining assistance needed by the group—a crafts instructor, for example. All of the recreation-type activities will probably be in one activity component. These would include active games/sports, arts and crafts, hobbies, drama, and music. They should all meet at the same time or on the same day. Meeting on different days may cause conflicts with other church activities. In fact, the church may have a recreation program which already provides these activities for all ages. If so, the club will not need to make additional provisions.

Arts and crafts for senior adults should be no different than those for other adults. However, senior adults may be more willing to make things from available materials. Those who have had to make-do for most of their lives are more creative with available materials. Rather than listing the many crafts ideas which are available, ask your senior adults for their suggestions in addition to what they have indicated on the survey. Any needed instructors should be enlisted from your senior adult group if possible. One other note: In all the arts and crafts programs I have observed, the senior adults pay for materials which have to be purchased. However, if your church pays for recreation materials and equipment for other age groups, then you would want to do the same for senior adults.

A hobby group or groups may be planned for those already engaged in a hobby and others who wish to become involved in specific hobbies. These groups may be small and should have a leader from their own number. A specific time should be set for hobby groups to meet so they do not become a little club of their own.

Arts, crafts, and hobbies groups should be encouraged to display their work occasionally at general meetings.

Senior adults appear to be increasingly interested in drama and music. Skits and brief dramatic presentations may be studied, rehearsed, and presented in general meetings, other church events, and in ministry activities. A new book of short plays, *Drama for Senior Adults* by Sarah Walton Miller, is a good resource. A senior adult musical, "Count On Us," is available from Light Hearted Publishing Company, P. O. Box 15246, in Nashville, Tennessee. This full-length musical, to be sung and performed by senior adults, was written by Sarah Walton Miller and Don Madaris. I recommend it to you as a special project through your church music ministry and/or senior adult club.

Another activity component of your club could be trips. The chairman of that component and others whom he may enlist will plan the trips. Some senior adult clubs plan a trip a month. These are usually one-day trips to a place of interest not too far away. Such trips include: special gardens, museums, capitol buildings, denominational headquarters, mission points, hospitals, nursing homes, a farm, a lake, a park, a theater production, a concert, a ball game, a school, another church, a conference, a convention, a beach, a fair or carnival, a shopping center, a factory, an airport. Occasionally longer trips may be planned. Some have gone to theme parks (Opryland, Disney World, Six Flags over Texas), national parks, cruises in the Caribbean, Hawaii, Nova Scotia, Williamsburg, Europe, and the Holy Land. Obviously the longer trips cost more money and will be limited to those who can afford to participate.

Successful trip planning is quite detailed, including some special precautions. You will need to know:

• where you are going
• how long it will take to get there
• the best means of transportation for the particular trip
• where and when you will eat and sleep overnight (make reservations)
• what the total cost will be.

For senior adults you will need to:

• be prepared for emergency health needs
• be sure the place you're going is easily accessible
• plan not to travel too long each day
• have a definite schedule of activities but do not crowd the days.

Retreats have already been mentioned in the discussion of spiritual enrichment, but they are also needed for socialization purposes. They should be planned by special committees appointed by the president or by the executive committee of the club. The coordinator should work closely with the officers in planning such events. A sample agenda appears in the Appendix.

Many churches have an annual retreat for their own senior adults. The senior adults in the Hunter Street Baptist Church in Birmingham, Alabama, requested two retreats per year. One is led by the pastor and staff. An outside guest is invited to be the speaker at the other. In some area associations, churches plan joint retreats as do some state denomination groups.

Southern Baptists conduct Chautauquas (senior adult conferences named for the early adult education movement originated at Lake Chautauqua, New York) at their conference centers in New Mexico and North Carolina each fall. Nazarene International Retreats of Golden Agers are held in several places in the United States and Canada by the Church of the Nazarene. These enlarged retreats provide opportunity for socialization with persons from all over the nation in worship, Bible study, recreation, and fellowship.

Other activities include banquets and parties. For special occasions such as holidays, banquets could be planned by senior adults themselves. To foster intergenerational fellowship, senior adults could plan and conduct banquets for other ages such as youth or young adults. An added feature for a banquet for younger adults would be child care—either in the couples' homes or at the church. Parties for children would be a variation of this activity. For such events, the president should appoint temporary committees.

Activities in the recreational area include active sports. A fishing rodeo, golf tournament, senior adult men's softball team, bowling team or tournament—all would probably attract men, and some women would also be interested. These activities would be carried out by leaders appointed from those interested in these activities, unless they are a part of the church recreation program.

Summary

Any kind of social activity provided will attract some senior adults. Be careful to provide the balance of activities required in your church to supply the socialization interests and needs of your senior adults. As attractive as some programs may appear in other churches, it is not wise for you to duplicate them for your church unless you are sure your senior adults want them.

SERVICE OPPORTUNITIES

Most churches have not begun to tap the potential resources in their older members. Some churches have recognized their value and involved them in meaningful service opportunities.

It is difficult to divide clearly the responsibility for service opportunity between the church and a senior adult club. Of course, churches will approach these matters differently. The primary concern is that the purpose of meaningful involvement be accomplished. The senior adult council should consider carefully the following suggestions and determine what should be done by the church's service ministries, leaving other possibilities to the discretion of the club.

Ongoing Church Programs

Naturally, the church should consider senior adults to fill teaching, leadership, and support positions in working with their peers as well as with other ages. Sometimes senior adults will suggest that they be replaced by younger persons in places of leadership. These have succumbed to the retirement syndrome discussed earlier. Basic program leaders should encourage senior adults who ought to remain in service. Many are superior in their knowledge and skills, and your church cannot afford to lose their ministry.

Individual Service Opportunities

Often a senior adult can provide an individual service which would be more difficult for a younger person. For example, a large downtown church needed surrounding property for expansion. Efforts to obtain the property had failed. Finally, one of the church trustees, a retired real estate man, volunteered to pursue the matter. Using his former contacts, his skills, and wisdom, he succeeded in acquiring two pieces of property which soon led to other property becoming available, more than doubling the land area owned by the church.

Some other general services which may be rendered by senior adults include: financial and other record keeping; general office work; lawn care; flower arranging; building maintenance and repairs; operating a benevolence closet/pantry; operating a health equipment loan closet; helping in the kitchen with food service; providing library services; serving as prayer warriors; providing a tape ministry; visiting shut-ins, the institutionalized and newcomers; leading new member orientation; and providing transportation, counseling, and assistance to senior adults and younger persons.

Many of these service opportunities occur when specific persons are invited to perform specific responsibilities.

Organized Services to Others

Senior adults also need services performed for them. One of the most important services to be provided to senior adults is *referral to resources for meeting their needs*. Earlier, I suggested that the task force which conducted the survey of the senior adults and initiated the senior adult ministry also make an inventory of the resources available in the community to assist older persons with their needs. A file of such resources is primary to the provision of a referral service. Information is filed by need headings and also alphabetically.

A church in Dallas, Texas, and another in Saint Louis, Missouri, have referral services. They provide manned desks during certain hours of the week. The senior adults at those desks are familiar with the resources and can direct those in need to the source best able to meet particular needs.

The person or persons responsible for this service should constantly seek out new resources, be an advocate for senior adults with agencies which provide help, and have a genuine interest in following through to see that persons who are referred do receive assistance. If the referral service worker is well acquainted with personnel in agencies, their phone call to advise the agency of the referral is helpful. They may even introduce the referred person on the telephone so that the initial contact will be made that way.

In your club organization, one person or a committee could have this responsibility. This activity could be a part of the service opportunities component.

Telephone reassurance is a vital service rendered by some senior adult groups. It meets the need of the person who lives alone or with someone who is incapacitated. That need is to have the assurance that someone cares and that, if something were to happen to him, someone would soon know and provide help.

The system usually operates with someone accepting an assignment to call daily a person or a few people who have expressed a desire for this service. The calls are made at a prearranged time. If there is no answer, and there has not been previous notice that the one being called would not be at home, some plan of checking on the person is put into effect. In some places the fire department or police department has accepted the responsibility for checking. In others, volunteers check on persons who live in their area. Sometimes church staff persons assume that responsibility. A variation is to have the persons being served call in rather than being called.

This service relieves anxiety and provides a daily contact with interested persons outside the home. Creative names given to the service include Care-Ring, which is descriptive of the service.

Senior adults may operate this service for their church members and others. The first step is to enlist people who will make the calls. Then those who have expressed an interest in being called should be contacted. The program may be publicized so that others may enroll also. Assignments are made to callers who make an initial contact with those to be called and establish a procedure for daily calling.

The seriousness of this project should be impressed upon both the callers and the called. Those being called need to understand that an emergency plan will go into effect if they do not answer, so they should inform their caller if they plan to be away at a specific time. The callers must realize that those being called are dependent upon them and that the assurance being sought will be destroyed if the callers are not faithful.

The friendly visitors program operates much like the telephone reassurance except that it is personal contact in the homes and may not be daily. The visitor may take items to the visited, such as decorations from the club meetings, church bulletins, and personal favors. The visitor may provide services such as reading mail, writing letters, assisting in shopping, and, perhaps most importantly, listening.

Many churches have a ministry to shut-ins or homebound persons as a part of their Sunday School program. Work to make yours effective. You may then not need the friendly visitors program. On the other hand, it could well be a complement to that service, especially if it can be a neighborly, informal visit by one who has genuine interest and time. If your church chooses to do both, then the friendly visitors program must coordinate with that of the Sunday School.

Organization and operation of the program will be similar to that described for the telephone reassurance project. A plan for reporting visits and news from those being visited would strengthen the program considerably. Remember, it would be better for the homebound person to not anticipate a visit than to anticipate one and be disappointed.

Shopping assistance is another service mobile senior adults may provide to those who have no transportation or who cannot see well enough to select items. Much of this kind of ministry is being provided informally by neighbors, friends, and family members. But there are those who still have no one to assist them, and they are reluctant to ask. The service can best be provided by informal arrangements between one who is willing to serve and one or more who have the need. Informal reporting of news from those being served would be of interest to the club. To provide continuing service where persons may find they can no longer serve, assign a person or committee designated to operate this project.

Closely tied to shopping assistance and a major need of many senior adults is *transportation.* Many senior adults who drive their own cars are willing to provide transportation to others to attend meetings at the church. Some will also be willing to take people to shopping malls, the doctor's office, the dentist's office, or other places. Again, this can be an informal arrangmement made between two or more persons, or it can be a structured service. Assign a person and place for those who need transportation to call, and schedule it. Further details of a plan for transportation are given in the next section of this chapter, "Services Needed."

Home repairs is another opportunity for service involvement. The plan usually functions by putting those who need minor home repairs in touch with those who have the skills to perform the repair. This service would be for those who can no longer do such things for themselves—for example, women who live alone or men physically disabled. Usually the one receiving the service pays for all materials. A plan for payment or volunteer work should be arranged ahead of time.

The First Baptist Church of Ferguson, Missouri, and some other local churches are providing a home repair service through their senior adult clubs. If this service is included in your club activities, a clearing point or person needs to be established for relating those with needs to those who will assist. Your survey likely indicated someone who has an interest in this area who would accept the responsibility. Issue a request to your group for volunteers to provide assistance. Those who have indicated a need for home repairs should be contacted. Implement the program by assigning the needs to the volunteer helpers. As a matter of interest, reports should be made through the service opportunities component chairman to the officers of the club for their report to the general meetings. Of course, if your club is not this structured, time should be given in your general meeting for sharing these kinds of activities.

The home repair project could be expanded to allow senior adults to *use other vocational and avocational skills in helping others.* For example, a retired accountant might help others who need answers to tax questions. A retired business person could serve as a consultant to younger persons just beginning in business. You can think of many other possibilities.

Many senior adults have an interest in *gardening*, both vegetable and flowers. Some community programs for older persons have included gardening as one of their projects, making a plot available to an older person or a couple to grow things for themselves. The Harrisburg Baptist Church in Tupelo, Mississippi, set aside a part of their property for such use by their senior adult club.

Mature Living magazine carries regular feature articles on gardening for senior adults. Cooperative Extension Service agents will provide such services as soil testing, advice on seed and plant selection, and solutions to problems.

This seasonal service can be extended into a year-long activity if the group becomes a hobby group, raising plants both indoors and outdoors and engaging in studies on the subject. A leader for this group should be found easily among your members.

Senior adults can *provide special activities for others.* Many of these would be social in nature and could be provided to shut-ins, institutionalized, handicapped, day care, and other groups. Some clubs have entertainment groups like the Kitchen Band of the Swope Park Baptist Church in Kansas City. These groups provide entertainment and social activities regularly for others. Have small groups take decorations, food, and entertainment from your general meetings to those who cannot attend. For one of your general meetings or a special meeting, make special provisions for attendance by those who cannot attend regularly.

Many nursing home and other long-term care institution residents are able to get out occasionally and need this contact to maintain orientation with the outside world. You may wish to plan an outing to provide them an opportunity to be outside. Such events as these may be special projects for which special committees are appointed, or you may wish to have a person or committee responsible for planning and carrying out such activities throughout the year. One idea for making this a continuing service is to adopt a nursing home or other institution and plan activities for a year, including holidays and other special events. You will need to establish a definite working relationship with the administration of the institution, recognizing their responsibility for the residents. In some cases it may also be advisable to consult with the families of the institutionalized before planning outside trips.

Community Service Opportunities

Under this heading of service opportunities, suggestions have been made of ways the church can utilize the time, talents, and interests of retired persons through the club organization. There are also opportunities for your senior adults to share in the community through special organizations. Many of the nutrition programs under the various titles of the Older Americans' Act and other locally funded programs use volunteers. Many senior adults have found personal satisfaction in these opportunities of fellowship and serving as well as receiving. Some deliver meals to the homebound, serve tables, keep records, provide transportation, entertain, and counsel.

Volunteer programs sponsored by the federal agency Action include the Retired Senior Volunteer Program (RSVP), the Senior Corps of Retired Executives (SCORE), Foster Grandparents, and Volunteers in Service to America (VISTA). RSVP serves to find volunteer jobs in the community for senior adults who would like to serve. SCORE matches retirees with technical, professional, and business skills with small businesses which need consultation and advice. Foster Grandparents pays a small stipend to older persons enlisted to work with children, usually in mental health institutions. VISTA is also a program which pays a small stipend to persons involved in services to help the poor. A relatively new feature of that program is to use locally recruited senior adults in some projects. Senior Companions is the latest of the programs under ACTION and serves older persons in their homes or in institutions in a manner similar to the friendly visitors project described earlier. Information on these public programs may be obtained from your state agency on aging or your area agency on aging. Obtain those names and addresses through the governor's office of your state.

Other opportunities for service in the community may be found through the Volunteer Action Committee if there is one in your city. Many schools, libraries, and other public programs are happy to have retirees as volunteers for a variety of services.

Senior adults interested in service involvement in the community should also be referred to the various agencies by your club's referral service.

Summary

Officers of a very successful senior adult club in the First Baptist Church in Springfield, Missouri, attended a conference on aging in which ministry opportunities were discussed. The president of that group remarked that she had been concerned that the glow had dimmed in their organization. Now she understood that they had neglected the need to provide service opportunities as well as opportunities for socialization and recreation. A balanced program of ministry with senior adults in your church must provide for giving as well as receiving.

SERVICES NEEDED

It is impossible to discuss service opportunities without describing services needed by other senior adults. It is important, however, that we look at these services and others from the perspective of those who are in need.

Through Ongoing Programs

Every church provides some ministry to older persons through its ongoing activities. No church should be neglecting its homebound and institutionalized members. Surely pastoral care is given older persons as it is to other ages, if not more so. There is natural support by church members who are neighbors, by members of organized classes, and by highly motivated Christian individuals. Your Sunday School has the general task of ministry to its members and prospects. Above this, however, your survey probably has revealed indications of many needs which the church should consider meeting. The missions organizations should accept responsibility for some of these through their mission action programs.

Referrals to Agencies

Knowing about available resources, encouraging senior adults to accept those resources, and counseling senior adults with problems should perhaps be the first order of ministry. The church can provide this assistance through its active senior adults as described earlier, the church office, or another organization or committee. Concern for individuals and a desire to be helpful should motivate church leaders to be aware of any source of help for persons in need. Yet many ministers are not aware of Supplemental Security Income, a federal program administered by the Social Security Administration, guaranteeing a minimum scale of living income for all persons age 65 or older. That has been a basic provision which has been highly publicized for years. The many other programs are too numerous to list here but can be discovered through the inventory of community resources suggested in chapter 3.

Before you begin to compile an extensive file, determine if there is an effective referral service already established in your community. If there is, channel your older persons through that service. In referring a senior adult to the referral service or to a specific agency, it will be helpful in many cases if someone who is knowledgeable escorts the older person to the resource and assists him.

Counseling

An elderly acquaintance told me about his concern over a city ordinance which had required him to do extensive repairs on some old houses he owned. I called the city authority who was enforcing the ordinance and found that my friend had been given two extensions of time and that there was no choice but to prosecute. When I explained to the older man that nothing really could be done, he replied, "I am so old and so tired. I wish I had someone to make this decision for me." Of course I would not have presumed to usurp his independence by telling him what to do. But I did help him think through the whole matter and reach the decision to sell the property and invest his money in some other way.

This kind of counseling in the face of problems often helps older persons. The church could have designated persons, perhaps retired business and professional people, to provide this ministry on a regular basis. Many pastors do this, but their time is limited. Many older persons would not want to "bother them."

Provisions for Special Needs

Transportation is among the most frequently mentioned needs of senior adults. Many communities and groups seek to relieve this problem. Strangely enough, some of those programs are failing because of lack of riders. When there is the need and a provision for meeting that need, failure of the program is usually due to lack of communication. Would-be riders are unaware of the service, or they do not accept it as legitimate or adequate for them. The church can enter such a situation as an advocate to make the program work. Frequently, older persons will be more accepting if the church gives its approval.

Regardless of the provision by the community, there will be transportation needs which the church should meet. Those provisions may range from running a dial-a-ride program with minibuses to an informal volunteer provision of rides as requested to specific places or activities. A plan for receiving requests and enlisting drivers needs to be implemented. A file of volunteers indicating their availability and the extent to which they will provide transportation could be maintained by an individual who is accessible for requests for transportation. That person then could call the volunteers to see if they could meet the need at hand.

In a northeastern state a transportation program was reported to have been run by a lady permanently confined to her bed in her home. She did it all by telephone.

Mental and physical health needs are higher among older persons, mainly because their conditions are most often chronic. Lack of incentive to get help, inadequate finances, and poor nutrition practices contribute to poor health. As the church provides activities with senior adults, their meaning in life becomes more evident, and their incentive to be well increases. Socialization, particularly those activities which include food, encourages those who live alone to eat more properly. Discussions and studies in health practices, physical fitness, budgeting, and nutrition will prove helpful. Grocery shopping assistance by someone who can help plan meals will also improve nutrition habits.

The church can provide opportunities for health screening and other preventive health activities through its senior adult club activities. Medical doctors and nurses may be enlisted as volunteers, or you may seek the assistance of the public health department. Many health needs will come to your attention, which must be referred to others who are prepared to meet such needs.

Economic need is listed as the number one need in national surveys of older persons. The church will probably not be in a position to provide financial assistance but can refer persons to possible re-sources. Your program can include studies and suggestions on how to stretch the dollars which retired persons do have. Home economists, utility company representatives, bankers, and others will be willing to help.

Employment is related to economic need but also a concern of some who are bored in retirement. Again, referrals may be made to proper agencies. Some cities have offices established specifically to help retirees find employment.

The church may wish to set an example by considering older persons for some of their employed positions. One church voted a salary of $10,000 a year for an assistant pastor. When a qualified person could not be found for that salary, the pastor enlisted ten retired persons to work part-time for $1,000 each per year. That provided each additional income, did not affect their Social Security or other retirement programs, and gave them meaningful involvement while providing their church many times the service that would have been possible by the addition of one staff person.

Nutrition was mentioned in connection with health. Because it is so critical to the well-being of any person, it should be considered separately. The required daily amount of food for an older person may be less than for a younger person, but the basic vitamins and minerals are still required. Federal, state, and locally funded programs of meals for senior adults in group settings, or home delivered, have proliferated in the last few years. Any older person who does not eat properly is eligible to participate and should be encouraged to do so. Most of the programs provide for some payment of meals if the individual is capable. This removes the stigma attached to a "free meal." Nutrition education should consciously be provided through the various opportunities with senior adults in the church.

In his address to the White House Conference on Aging in 1971, the president stated that we must provide those programs and services necessary to allow older persons to continue to live in their own *homes* or other places of residence of their choosing as long as possible. He expressed the feeling of most persons who want to remain in their own home instead of moving to some living environment totally different from that to which they have been accustomed.

The barrier to many continuing to live in their homes is their inability to maintain their houses in a way which was once possible. Even with money, many cannot obtain the services of craftsmen to do minor repairs and maintenance. Recently some community agencies have begun to make some such provision. For example, some funding has been given to winterize homes. Some employment agencies have added the service of providing names of retired tradesmen who will perform those kinds of services at a nominal cost.

Another barrier to some older persons remaining in their own home is their inability to perform heavy homemaker chores. Most county social service agencies provide some homemakers who do such things as the heavy cleaning, laundry, and maybe some cooking. These services are limited, of course, because of lack of personnel and heavy demand, but they should be available to those who have extreme need.

Through organizations such as the mission groups of women and younger persons, your church might be able to meet some such needs of its members. Diplomacy and tact must be exercised in providing such ministry to one who has not specifically asked for it. For those whose survey cards indicate the need, there should be ready acceptance.

Living alone in virtual isolation increases the *anxiety* of older persons. Their question is, "What would happen to me if I should fall and injure myself and not be able to get to a telephone?" The telephone reassurance program is a fairly simple solution to that problem. It is described in detail in the preceding section on service opportunities. It, of course, could be operated by the church in other ways.

A professional way of meeting this need is to use an answering service which either calls the older person or receives a daily call from him. This method may cause loss of the personal interaction engendered by other methods.

Alternative housing is the need which faces many older persons. Without discussing the possibility of your church's maintaining housing for senior adults, consider ways in which the church may be helpful. Investigate available housing in your area. Hopefully this housing will range in levels of care from self-help to protective care to intermediate health care and, finally, to skilled nursing care. With these alternatives available, determine the level needed by the individual. Counsel the person to maintain himself or to be maintained at the lowest level of care required as long as possible. Families of older persons will need counsel at this point, too. Studies and discussion groups on the subject should be scheduled to reduce the shock which comes when a loved one must leave the old home and enter other housing environments. The church should be concerned about the quality of housing and care provided in its community and serve as an advocate for quality. This can be achieved best by establishing positive, helpful relationships with administrations which lead to trust and mutual respect.

Summary

It is in the area of needed services that most churches will be the weakest in providing ministry with senior adults. A balanced program of ministry with senior adults in your church, however, must consider those who are freqently invisible to your congregation. We must not allow them to be "out of sight, out of mind" or "to be neither seen nor heard."

I'm not an advocate of the church providing for all the senior adults' needs. I do recommend stronger working relationships between community services and the church. We must be concerned, and our concern must result in action. More often that action will take the form of obtaining a service which is provided outside of the church. Still there remains those things which the church can do best. Look closely at the suggestions made in these last two sections of this chapter as you consider the discovered need of senior adults in your church and plan a balanced program to meet that need.

Summary and Conclusion to Part III

A great deal of material has been provided in Part III. You should be encouraged to see the many things which can be done and the variations of persons, circumstances, programs, and needs which can be considered in producing a comprehensive program of ministry with senior adults in your church. Remember, you do not have to do everything; but you must be faithful in providing those things needed and requested insofar as it is possible.

PART IV
Enlarging Your Vision

10

Accept the Challenge: Evaluate and Expand Your Senior Adult Ministry

It is said of coaches that they are never content with the accomplishments of their teams. Can any less be said of our mission to minister with senior adults? The challenge is there! We have the whole person with whom and to whom to minister—spiritual, social, mental, and physical. Apply that to each individual senior adult whom your church could possibly reach, and it is obvious that the work will never be totally completed. We probably have just begun to see the possibilities of this work. 1 Corinthians 2:9, taken somewhat out of context, seems appropriate here: "But as it is written, Eye hath not seen, nor ear heard, neither hath entered into the heart of man, the things which God hath prepared for them that love him."

So where do you go from here? When you have gone through the process described up to this point, what do you do next?

EVALUATE!

Evaluate Your Planning

How well have you done with the plans for developing a ministry with senior adults? Examine the steps in the plan outlined on the first chart in chapter 3. Did your church experience motivation? Did your plan result in the actions outlined?

If you discover any weaknesses, make supplementary plans to strengthen the overall process by accomplishing the *whats* not done previously.

113

Evaluate Your Objectives

The objectives you set to establish the direction for your ministry with senior adults should be used, also, to evaluate that ministry. Review the list of suggested objectives and the discussion of those objectives in chapter 5. As you consider your progress toward achieving your objectives, review those objectives in the light of your experience to this point. Revise them as appropriate. The level of achievement of each of your objectives will help you establish priorities and develop immediate strategies to accomplish what you set out to do.

Evaluate Your Club

The Standard of Excellence provided here may be used as a checklist for evaluating your club. The requirements are minimum. Every point should be achieved and a standard rating should be maintained. Having accomplished this much, your club should not be content with bare minimum achievements.

Standard of Excellence

I. Organization
   1. The church has elected a coordinator for senior adult ministry.
   2. Senior adults have elected officers for the club. The officers are a president, a vice-president, and a secretary.
   3. The president of the club plus representatives from senior adult activities in other church programs comprise a senior adult council. The senior adult coordinator is chairman of this council and represents its work to the church council in the same way that other such councils are represented.
   4. The coordinator has attended a special senior adult leadership seminar, conference, or workshop provided by the denomination at a national, state, or local opportunity.
   5. Every senior adult in the church is eligible to be a member. (Age 60 years and older is generally accepted as a definition for senior adults.)
II. Planning
   1. The senior adult club officers and activity component chair-

man plan club meetings and activities three to twelve months in advance.

2. The senior adult council meets at least annually to coordinate activities planned by the club and the various other programs of the church and to plan the overall church activities for senior adults.

3. Meetings and activities are publicized through the church bulletin, newsletter, mail-outs, a yearbook, or other available means.

4. Preretirees are provided information about the senior adult ministry and other helps for their preparation for retirement.

5. Regular contact is made with senior adults who may be ill. This is in close cooperation with the Homebound Department of the Sunday School and other home visitation programs.

6. Contact and regular sharing of information is maintained with others in the community who serve the elderly.

III. Programming
1. Programs and activities deal with senior adult concerns in five basic areas: spiritual enrichment, learning opportunities, socialization, service opportunities, and services needed.

2. All programming for senior adults is coordinated with and channeled through appropriate church programs.

3. Classes or study courses using special books prepared for senior adults are conducted at least annually.

4. The club sponsors at least one trip per year. (The trip does not have to be overnight.)

5. The church celebrates an annual Senior Adult Day or week.

IV. Promoting
1. Participation in area, state, and national senior adult activities is encouraged.

2. Special periodicals for senior adults, such as *Mature Living* magazine, are promoted by frequent announcements and by at least occasional programs based on material found in them.

3. Senior adults are encouraged to read special books prepared for them by the denomination and other life-enrichment materials available through the church or community library.
4. Senior adults are advised of continuing education opportunities provided in the area or by correspondence.
5. The senior adult club promotes active participation in all of the programs and special activities of the church.

V. Reporting and Evaluating
1. The senior adult coordinator reports to the church at least annually on the total senior adult ministry. The report is prepared by the senior adult council for the church council.
2. The effectiveness of the senior adult club is evaluated each year, and a report is made to the council. The council evaluates each major church senior adult activity after its completion and reports to the church council for further evaluation.
3. The results of evaluations are used to revise and strengthen any weaknesses noted in the program.

Evaluate Your Effectiveness

The effectiveness of your ministry with senior adults will be measured primarily by observation. This evaluation is highly subjective but is important to your overall measurement of success.

Here are ten areas in which improvement is desirable. Use these as evaluation points for the effectiveness of your senior adult ministry. Look for these in your senior adults:
1. Real life satisfaction (as opposed to "lip" satisfaction)
2. Purpose in participation (as opposed to activity for activity's sake)
3. Expectation (outlook and attitude toward the future)
4. Self-confidence
5. Independent action
6. Competence (ability to achieve)
7. Creativity (dare to try)
8. Physical health
9. Motivation (initiative)

10. Carryover to other programs (friendships and services to others).

Ideally, with adequate and properly trained leadership, each senior adult would be periodically evaluated by these and/or other points. At least be aware of these desirable traits; observe your groups to see if your programs are effective, and improve in these traits.

EXPAND!

Expand Your Attendance

The number of senior adults attending club activities is an indicator for evaluating success. Be careful to consider the potential number of participants lest you become satisfied with a comfortable number. In one church, the leadership was excited to have approximately three hundred participating in their varied activities. Following a suggestion that they determine their total potential, they discovered more than eight hundred senior adults in their church membership. Regularity of attendance and participation should be a constant concern. A review of the section on membership in chapter 6 will be helpful at this point.

The most important consideration in building attendance is a well-planned program. If it offers activities in which your senior adults are interested and for which they have a felt need, it will be attractive. Information and suggestions given in Part III, chapters 7, 8, and 9, provide a variety of activities to appeal to all of your senior adults.

When your club has been in operation for about six months, look at your survey cards again to see if individuals are responding to those activities in which they had expressed an interest. Try to determine if there are barriers to attendance, such as lack of transportation or escort, which you may help remove. As you look at the other cards of nonparticipants, look for keys to getting these persons involved. Some will come only if given a specific assignment. You may not be offering anything of specific interest to others. A few may still not be aware that the program is for them. And it should be said again that some will have no need or desire for the program; they do not need to be harassed. Some will need to have their interest cultivated. A senior adult acquaintance who is actively involved in the program can do this cultivation best.

To increase participation, make announcements before groups, use public information time on radio and television, print promotions in newsletters and newspapers. Maintain contact by individual visits. Remember, some will need to be cultivated by carefully gaining their confidence and friendship, which often takes time and repeated contacts.

Any approach you take should carefully explain the purpose of the program. Explain who the program is for, that it is informal (nonthreatening, noncompetitive, nonembarrassing), and that there is no cost. Caution those who work with you not to be demanding. A principle of this adult program is that persons may participate as they desire and at the levels which they wish.

Perhaps another word should be said about involving individuals in the program. As stated earlier, some will attend only if given specific responsibilities. Many will drop out unless they are actively involved. Involvement may take many forms — from elected positions to simply making a suggestion which is accepted. As a reminder, reread those sections of earlier chapters which deal with involvement.

The club officers and the senior adult council should be concerned about those who do not attend or attend infrequently. The vice-president has specific responsibility for this area. As suggested in chapter 6, the vice-president may enlist individuals or a committee to assist with this responsibility. Actually, several committees could be formed if enough persons are involved. The committee work could be divided into publicity, telephone contacts, and visitation. If your club has its own newsletter, make it the assignment of the secretary, who in turn could have a committee for that purpose.

The club also has responsibility for senior adults who cannot attend. That responsibility will be shared with other programs of the church, such as a Homebound Ministry through the Sunday School and/or a deacon family ministry plan. Where these exist, close coordination and avoidance of duplication is necessary. The club can plan special activities for the homebound and institutionalized. These would include taking programs to them on special occasions and even taking something of the regular programs. For example, several members could visit a shut-in or a group in an institution immediately following the regular general meeting, taking refreshments, decorations, tape-recorded parts of the program, and written greetings from those who were in attendance.

Those who cannot attend should also be provided assistance to get to special events such as Senior Adult Day, a special church anniversary program, or other general celebrations.

Expand Your Activities

By closely observing those who participate and carefully analyzing the reasons given by those who do not participate, you will be better able to keep a balance in the activities your club offers. Some activities will run their course and need to be discontinued temporarily or even permanently. The discovery of new and additional interests will lead you to add activity components. Increasing and changing interests is an indication of an alive program with involved participation in planning, decision making, and implementation.

The procedure for adding new components is the same as for those begun originally. Find the person who is most interested in an activity and who will agree to serve as chairman of that component; determine the time and place for the activity; and publicize its availability to all of your senior adults.

Reviewing Part III, expecially chapter 9, will remind you of potential activities. It will also help you maintain a balance of activities in the five areas of concern. At some point your church may be interested in going beyond those suggestions to some other structured ministries. Some have even considered the following: day-care services, a nutrition program with meals served at the church, a health clinic, an employment service, adopted grandparents, legal services, and housing. In many communities these services are already provided by other agencies. So I repeat my concern that you not seek to duplicate services which are already being provided effectively. If you are still interested in these possibilities, write: Senior Adult Ministry Section, Family Ministry Department, Sunday School Board of the Southern Baptist Convention, 127 Ninth Avenue, North, Nashville, TN 37234.

One other area of enlarged ministry is in joining with other churches in your area or association in the provision of services and activities for which larger support is more feasible. These kinds of activities include everything from the provision of specialized social services to the sharing in fellowship with a larger group or a joint retreat. Such activities may be arranged through formal structure or an informal representative committee for special activities. A director of missions, director of social ministries, or other staff persons in a local association of churches should be contacted in the interest of any joint ventures. Missions organizations such as Southern Baptists' Woman's Missionary Union and Brotherhood may be an avenue for this enlarged ministry. One important advantage of this arrangement is that small churches with few senior adults would have opportunities for activities which otherwise might not be possible.

Expand Information and Referral

In addition to the activities of your own ministry with senior adults, encourage your members to participate in other opportunities which are available. These include community-type programs which have been discussed in detail in chapter 9. There are also opportunities provided by your denomination. For Southern Baptists there is the National Association of Baptist Senior Adults. This individual-membership organization informs its members regularly of all denominational activities for senior adults through its newsletter, *The Gazette*. The association itself offers: several weeks of conferences, called Chautauquas, at the conference centers in Glorieta, New Mexico, and Ridgecrest, North Carolina; cruises; and tours. Other departments and agencies of the Southern Baptist Convention provide additional Bible study opportunities, missionary and service opportunities, and, in a cooperative effort, national conferences on aging.

Expand Your Facilities

As your senior adult ministry grows, you will need to be constantly aware of the adequacy of your facilities. Lack of adequate space for the program was the reason given by some senior adults for not attending senior centers.

Ideally, programs should shape facilities, but we often have to accommodate our program to existing facilities. Study all your available space so that what you have can be used to its maximum.

Keep in mind that space should be easily accessible for older persons. It should be well lighted and kept at a comfortable temperature. Floor surfaces should not be slippery; nor should they be covered with plush carpet. Any change in floor elevation should be readily observable, made so by good lighting and a marked change in colors. Furniture should be adult-size and chosen for comfort and utility. For example:

• Chairs should not be so low they are difficult to get into or out of.

• Tables for stand-up games should be high enough to not require stooping.

• Tables for sit-down games should be the proper height for the chairs being used so there is neither stretching up nor stooping over.

• Cabinets or tables on which materials are placed for senior adults to use should be high enough not to require stooping and low enough not to require stretching or standing on something in order to reach the height.

• Rest rooms should be convenient to the space being used and equipped for senior adults with the addition of handrails or bars for safety.

As you study your facilities, you may find that areas planned for the activities of other age groups may be modified easily to accommodate senior adults as well. A few churches may even find it feasible to build or renovate present buildings especially for weekday senior adult activities. Architects with experience in building facilities for older persons will be helpful in your planning facilities. Special information on activity space can be obtained from the Recreation Department of your denomination.

Expand Your Staff Support

As mentioned earlier, churches have a growing need to consider professional staff persons to direct their senior adult ministries. This ministry is highly specialized and requires special knowledge and skills. For this reason, special and continuing training for present church staff persons and volunteers is necessary. The highly specialized nature of the program may lead you to enlist the assistance of a professional consultant from your denomination to study and advise your church on its program.

Seminaries are becoming increasingly aware of the need to prepare professionals to enter the field of local church senior adult ministry. As your church evaluates and plans to expand its ministry with older persons, prayerfully consider the possibility of adding a staff person with that program responsibility.

Many of the needs of a senior adult ministry are being provided by staff persons with combinations of responsibility. The need still exists, though, for that combination staff person to get specialized training. As your church looks at its total ministry and considers staff persons to support that ministry, you should be concerned that the staff person who has senior adult responsibility has had special training for that purpose.

Expand Your Advocacy

The term *advocacy*, unfortunately, has fallen into misuse and misunderstanding. It is used here in a very positive, nonthreatening, nonmilitant sense. It does seem that the church has a responsibility in its community.

We should express our concern for poor housing, nutrition, income, institutions, inaccessible health care, transportation, security, and information. Your church may decide to form task groups to study these problems in the community and to report on them. Your church may adopt resolutions to be presented to the forums which are available to it and which have some power to make improvements.

Your church, perhaps through the senior adult council or club organization, should serve as an advocate between individual older members and agencies and organizations, helping with the resolution of problems of older persons. This should not be a demanding advocacy role but, rather, an accompanying of that older person to provide assistance with details and moral support. This kind of assistance may be provided by an organization or agency in your community. If so, the church would merely assist in establishing a relationship between the older person and that advocate organization.

Look to the Future

The complexion of the senior adult population is changing rapidly. Needs and interests of senior adults today will not likely be the same for the senior adults of the future. Similarities of persons born within the same ten-year span of time was discussed in chapter 1. For example, there are noticeable differences in the present senior adult groups and those which will immediately succeed them. Educational levels, economic conditions, life-styles, expectations, previous experiences, and value systems of those born in the 1920s and 30s will likely dictate considerable change in the senior adult ministries of local churches. As these differences emerge, your church is challenged to evaluate constantly and enlarge its provision for senior adults.

Some predict that some of the critical needs of senior adults today will be nonexistent for those of the future. Others believe older persons will always have those needs but that new ways of meeting them will be necessary.

I choose not to predict — except to say that there will be constant change. I am persuaded that the needs beyond those identified by Maslow as physiological will always be a concern of the church.

Our challenge is to be aware, understanding, concerned, and action-oriented toward the end that all senior adults may experience the abundant life promised by our Lord (John 10:10) and life with dignity and meaning in relation to others.

APPENDIX

A SCHEDULE FOR
DEVELOPING A SENIOR ADULT MINISTRY
(Sample)

TIME FRAME	ACTION	RESOURCE
	To Begin	
September	Church Decides to Enter the Process	Chapter 3
	Schedule the Special Emphasis Month	
	Elect a Senior Adult Coordinator	
October	Form the Task Force	
	Orient the Task Force	
November	Task Force Plans Special Emphasis Month	
January	Task Force Inventory Community Resources (1)	
February	Enlist Church Survey Captains (2)	
	Prepare Survey Materials	Chapter 4
	Make a List of All Senior Adults	
	Enter Information on Survey Forms (3)	
	Package Forms for Interviewers	
	Enlist Interviewers	
March	Publicize Senior Adult Emphasis Month	
	Pastor Writes All Senior Adults	
April	Senior Adult Emphasis Month	
(Last three	Sunday 1—''Church Awareness'' (5)	Chapter 1
Sundays)	Sunday 2—''Church Understanding'' (5)	Chapter 3
	Instruct and assign interviewers (4)	Chapter 4
	Begin survey	

	Sunday 3—"Church Concern" (5)	Chapter 3
	Survey Completed	Chapter 4
	Tabulate Results	
May	*Determine Direction*	Chapter 5
(First Sunday)	Sunday 4—"Church Commitment"	
	(Senior Adult Day) (5)	
	Senior Adult Lunch and Meeting (6)	
	Report Survey Results	
	Decide on Directions	
	Set First Meeting	
Last of May	*Organize a Senior Adult Ministry*	Chapter 6
June—July	*Plan a Balanced Program*	Chapters 7, 8, 9
September— October	*Evaluate and Expand*	Chapter 10

(1) Suggested form—page 126
(2) Smaller churches may not need
(3) Suggested form—page 127
(4) List of Instructions—page 47
(5) Suggestions—page 129 ff.
(6) An alternative would be to have a senior adult rally one day during the week, with inspiration, entertainment, refreshments and the survey report presented with discussion on recommended directions for a program.

COMMUNITY RESOURCES INVENTORY FORM

Primary Service_____

Agency Name_____

Contact Person_____

Address_____Phone_____

_____

Other Services_____

_____

_____

Eligibility Requirements_____

_____

SENIOR ADULT
NEEDS and INTERESTS SURVEY

General Information
1. Age Last Birthday

0 ____ 60-64

0 ____ 65-74

0 ____ 75 and over

2. Marital Status

0 ____ Spouse Living

0 ____ Widowed

0 ____ Never Married

3. Church Participation ____

0 ____ Morning Worship ____

0 ____ Evening Worship ____

0 ____ Sunday School ____

0 ____ Church Training ____

0 ____ Mission Organizations ____

0 ____ Prayer Meeting ____

NAME ____

ADDRESS ____

____

BIRTH DATE ____

TELEPHONE ____

REMARKS: ____

____

____

____

____

____

____

____

Interviewed by ____
Date ____

10. Spiritual Enrichment   0

11. Weekday Bible Study ____ 0

12. Discussion and Prayer Group ____ 0

13. Book Studies ____ 0

14. Retreats ____ 0

15. Other Name ____ 0

20. Learning Opportunities   0

21. Religions ____ 0

22. Personal Enrichment ____ 0

23. Arts and Crafts ____ 0

24. Hobbies ____ 0

25. Manual Skills ____ 0

26. Current Events ____ 0

27. Other Name ____ 0

0   30. **Socialization**

0 _____ 31. Fellowship with Peers

0 _____ 32. Fellowship with Other Ages

0 _____ 33. Arts and Crafts
                Name_____

0 _____ 34. Hobby Groups
                Name_____

0 _____ 35. Music Activities

0 _____ 36. Drama

0 _____ 37. Table Games

0 _____ 38. Sports Participation
                Name_____

0 _____ 39. Trips

0 _____ 40. Retreats

0 _____ 41. Church Club

50. **Service Opportunities**   0

51. General Office Work_____ 0

52. Library Work   _____ 0

53. Lawn Work   _____ 0

54. Home Repairs   _____ 0

55. Transportation   _____ 0

56. Visit   _____ 0

57. Telephone   _____ 0

58. Teach Arts, Crafts,
        Hobbies   _____ 0

59. Witness   _____ 0

60. Music   _____ 0

61. Mission Work   _____ 0

62. Work with Youth   _____ 0

63. Work with Children _____ 0

64. Community
        Programs   _____ 0

---

70. **SERVICES NEEDED**

0 _____ 71. Transportation

0 _____ 72. Health

0 _____ 73. Finances

0 _____ 74. Employment

0 _____ 75. Nutrition

0 _____ 76. Housing

77. Home Repairs   _____ 0

78. Homemaker   _____ 0

79. Friendly Visits   _____ 0

80. Telephone
        Reassurance   _____ 0

81. Shopping
        Assistance   _____ 0

82. Daycare   _____ 0

0 _____ 83. Other:_____

SUGGESTIONS FOR SENIOR ADULT EMPHASIS MONTH

Promote churchwide.

Pastor write all senior adult members.

Carry information for a month prior to and throughout the emphasis month in each edition of the church bulletin, newsletter, promotional sheet, or whatever avenues the church uses to promote activities. Publicize the special activities and inform about the senior adult years.

Plans for Sunday 1—*Awareness*

Ask each department of the Sunday School to have a special recognition of older persons. In younger departments have grandparents in attendance to assist with the regular and special activities. Youth and Adult Departments should have features on the number and potential of senior adults in the church and the community.

Recognize senior adults present in worship services. Inform the church of the numbers of senior adults in the church membership and Sunday School and of their participation in all the activities of the church.

Plans for Sunday 2—*Understanding*

Ask the Sunday School to plan to emphasize the importance of the senior years. Teachers in Youth and Adult Departments should deal with the myths of aging. Have someone state the facts of aging as stated in chapter 1.

In the worship service the pastor could preach on biblical teachings with reference to later life and old age (see chap. 2). The purpose of the sermon should be to help persons understand that old age is part of God's plan for persons as are the younger years.

Sunday 3—*Concern*

Ask Sunday School departments to consider projects through which interest in senior adults will be shown. These might be social activities with senior adults, ministry to a need of one or more senior adults (see chap. 9), or individual commitments through kind deeds for some older person.

The pastor could preach in the morning worship service on the responsibility of the church to minister to the whole person — with emphasis on older persons (see chap. 2).

Suggestions for Senior Adult Day

Seek to have every senior adult possible present for this day. Plan transportation, escort, and any other services necessary to get them there.

Begin the day with a time of fellowship. (Coffee, orange juice, and sweet rolls or doughnuts would be appropriate.) This could be a pre-session of the Sunday School. Register all who are present. Give them name tags and/or corsages and boutonnieres to wear for the day. (Senior adult stick-on cloth name badges are available from Baptist Book Stores.)

Use the senior adult Sunday School departments and classes for special features on the senior years. Someone could speak on the values, the challenges, or the joys of a long life. Appropriate Scripture verses could be quoted by several persons. Special application of the Sunday School content could be made to the senior adults, or a special study on Bible teachings on old age could be taught.

Senior adults should be encouraged to sit together in the morning worship service for special recognition. Some should serve as greeters and ushers. Others will be in the choir. Enlist some to participate in leading the service by reading Scripture, leading prayer, and giving a brief testimony. The pastor should preach on a subject related to old age. (See chap. 2 for Scripture suggestions.) If this is the day you are launching your senior adult ministry, the pastor may wish to preach on church commitment to minister to all persons, including the elderly. He should also lead the church to vote to approve a definite, conscious ministry with the senior adults of the church and community. Introduction of the senior adult coordinator would be appropriate at this time.

Lunch may be provided for senior adults immediately after the morning worship service. Youth or young adults may wish to serve.

This should not be a lengthy time. Make it light, entertaining, and enjoyable. (If this is the time you will report on the results of the survey of interest and needs, the coordinator should make this as informative as possible and lead senior adults to make decisions as discussed in chap. 5.)

The afternoon could be used to visit with senior adults who could not attend the church activities. Expressions of interest and love could be provided in the form of pot plants or other gifts. This may be done by the Homebound Departments of the Sunday School, senior adult volunteers, or others.

A history of your church would be an appropriate subject for presentation in the Church Training hour preceding the evening worship service. Or the senior adult department or group could begin a special church curriculum unit study on that night.

The evening service could include a musical presentation by senior adults. It could be a musical. (*Count on Us,* written by Sarah Walton Miller and Don Madaris, is available in Baptist Book Stores.) Or it could be a worship service of old hymns and brief devotional thoughts and testimonies by several senior adults.

Be careful to make the day one of celebration, honor, and appreciation. Avoid any negative portrayal of old age — even in attempted humor! Let there be nothing of condescension or charity. Planners and leaders of these activities should be very aware of the true facts of aging and the positive values of the later years.

(*Mature Living* magazine and other materials from the Senior Adult Section of the Family Ministry Department of the Sunday School Board of the Southern Baptist Convention will provide helps for senior adult day annually.)

A Senior Adult Retreat Program

A retreat is usually considered to be an overnight event in a setting conducive to activities planned and the atmosphere desired. The purpose of the senior adult retreat may be recreational (social), spiritual, educational, or any combination of these. Outsiders or local church leaders may make up the faculty for the retreat. (Retreats are referenced in chap. 9. The bibliography in the Appendix suggests sources for additional help in planning and conducting a retreat.)

A Sample Agenda

Theme: "Rightly Related to God and Man"

First Day

11:00 AM	Arrive at retreat site. Receive room assignments and unpack.
12:00 PM	Lunch and a program orientation.
1:00 PM	Rest or explore grounds.
2:00 PM	Bible study.
3:00 PM	Refreshments and break.
3:30 PM	Personal enrichment (Use the Broadman Press book *The Touch of Friendship* by Harold Dye)
4:30 PM	Free time
5:30 PM	Dinner
7:00 PM	Worship Service
	Scripture and prayer
	Drama by senior adults
	Song service
	Inspirational speaker
	Benediction
8:00 PM	Fellowship and refreshments

Second Day

6:30 AM	Morning watch — brief devotional message
7:00 AM	Breakfast
8:00 AM	Personal enrichment (*The Touch of Friendship*)
9:15 AM	Quiet sharing time by twos or threes
10:00 AM	Refreshment break
10:30 AM	Bible study
11:30 AM	Closing worship period
12:00 Noon	Lunch
1:00 PM	Free time
3:00 PM	Leave for home

Senior Adult Conference Program

A senior adult conference for a local church is similar to a retreat but is conducted at the church and adjusted to allow persons to return to their homes at night. Conferences would probably best be conducted in the daytime. An outside person or persons may be enlisted for presentations. The purpose will be to provide information and assistance to the participants. An appropriate book might be used as a basis for the content, or leaders may be enlisted to present information desired. For example, the conference could be on "The Community and Senior Adults" using persons representing their agencies and organizations such as Social Security, The American Association of Retired Persons, A Senior Center, The Local Council on an Area Agency on Aging. Invite other senior adults from the community to participate.

A Sample Agenda

Theme: The Community and Senior Adults

First Day

9:00 AM	Registration
9:15 AM	Devotional thoughts
9:30 AM	"Your Community Needs You"—The mayor
10:00 AM	Refreshment break
10:30 AM	Volunteer opportunities
	Panel of Retired Senior Volunteer Program (RSVP) director, librarian, hospital administrator, Boys Club leader, Red Cross leader
12:00 Noon	Lunch
1:00 PM	Fun time (organized games and activities)
2:30 PM	Refreshment break
3:00 PM	Important issues of your community
	Chamber of Commerce representative
	Public school administrator
	AARP leader
4:00 PM	Challenge to service—a senior adult
4:30 PM	Adjourn

Second Day

9:00 AM	Your community plan for serving senior adults—the director of the Area Agency on Aging
10:15 AM	Refreshment break
10:45 AM	A parade of resources (brief statements from leaders of Social Security, the Health Department, Social Services Agency, Medicaid, the local nutrition

program, the local senior center, the Cooperative
Extension Service)

12:00 Noon   Lunch
1:00 PM   Talk with the agencies (visit tables manned by
leaders of agencies)
2:30 PM   Refreshment break
3:00 PM   Challenge to use all available resources to maintain
health and a meaningful life
3:30 PM   Adjourn

Job Descriptions for Senior Adult Officers

Qualifications, responsibilities and training of all officers are discussed in chapter 6. These job descriptions may be helpful, too.

Senior adult coordinator

• Work closely with the pastor or other staff person as assigned
• Serve as chairman of the senior adult task force to determine needs and interests of senior adults in a church and establish the direction of the senior adult ministry of the church
• Serve as chairman of the senior adult council (formed after the task force has completed its work)
• Work closely with the senior adult club officers planning and conducting the various programs of the club
• Act as liaison between the club and the church, serving on the church council
• Act as liaison between all church programs serving senior adults
• Maintain relationships with community organizations serving the elderly
• Correlate and coordinate all activities of senior adults in the church through an annual calendar of activities developed by the senior adult council
• Report all senior adult activities to the church through regular church procedures
• Recommend actions for the church to take to enhance the senior adult ministry, such as building improvements, budgeting for special needs, special services to those in need, and churchwide features such as the annual Senior Adult Day

President of the club

- Work closely with the senior adult coordinator
- Lead the club executive committee, composed of officers and activity component chairmen, in planning general meetings and all other activities
- Preside over the regular general meetings
- Enlist activity component chairmen
- Appoint special committees as needed
- Serve on church committees as appropriate

Vice-President of the club

- Work closely with the president
- Serve on the executive committee of the club to plan the regular general meetings and all other activities
- Be responsible for enlisting senior adults to participate in club activities
- Be responsible for publicizing the activities of the club throughout the church and community
- Appoint and work with special committees as needed for promotion and publicity

Secretary of the club

- Work closely with the president and vice-president
- Serve on the executive committee of the club to plan regular general meetings and activities, keeping minutes of those meetings
- Be responsible for the registration of persons in attendance at regular general meetings
- Be responsible for greeting and fellowship opportunities for participants as they arrive for regular general meetings
- Appoint and work with special committees as needed for registration and pre-session time
- Prepare reports of general meetings for the executive committee
- Receive and maintain reports of the activity component chairmen

**SENIOR ADULT MINISTRY
ORGANIZATION CHART**

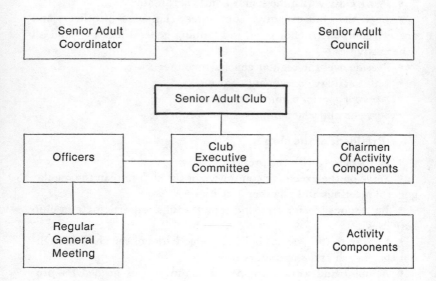

BIBLIOGRAPHY

Byrd, Annie Ward. *Can Senior Adults Be Saints?* Nashville: Convention Press, 1978.

Carlson, Adelle. *Life in the Senior Years.* Nashville: Convention Press, 1977.

Carlson, Adelle. *Senior Adult Weekday Get-Togethers.* Nashville: Broadman Press, 1975.

Cheavens, Alice Dawson. *It's OK to Be Yourself, Senior Adult.* Nashville: Convention Press, 1977.

Church Recreation Magazine. Nashville: The Sunday School Board of the Southern Baptist Convention.

Clingan, Donald F. *Aging Persons in the Community of Faith.* Saint Louis: Christian Board of Publication, 1975.

Cole, W. Douglas. *Working with Senior Adults in Sunday School.* Nashville: Convention Press, 1978.

Cook, Gary. *Retirees on Mission.* Memphis: Brotherhood Commission of the Southern Baptist Convention, 1978. (Produced jointly with Woman's Missionary Union, SBC, Birmingham.)

Cotton, Frank E., Jr. *Planning for the Aging: A Manual of Practical Methods.* Jackson: Mississippi Council on Aging, 1976.

Dunn, Jimmy F. *Developing Your Adult Church Training Program.* Nashville: Convention Press, 1977.

Dye, Harold E. *The Touch of Friendship.* Nashville: Broadman Press, 1979.

Ernst, Marvin, and Shore, Herbert. *Sensitizing People to the Processes of Aging: The In-Service Educator's Guide.* Denton, Texas: Center for Studies in Aging, North Texas State University, 1975.

Freeman, Carroll B. *The Senior Adult Years: A Christian Psychology of Aging.* Nashville: Broadman Press, 1979.

Gray, Robert M., and Moberg, David O. *The Church and the Older Person,* rev. ed. Grand Rapids: William B. Eerdmans Publishing Company, 1977.

Howell, C. John. *Senior Adult Family Life.* Nashville: Broadman Press, 1979.

Howell, Sarah. *Creative Crafts for Self-Expression.* Nashville: Broadman Press, 1978.

Jacobs, Belle. *Involving Them: A Challenge for Senior Citizens.* Washington: The National Council on the Aging, Inc., 1974.

Jordan, Joe J. *Senior Center Facilities: An Architect's Evaluation of Building Design, Equipment, and Furnishings.* Washington: The National Council on the Aging, Inc., 1975.

Kader, Raymond A. *Senior Adult Utilization and Ministry Handbook.* Nashville: Broadman Press, 1976.

Leanse, Joyce. *Senior Center: Report of Senior Group Programs in America.* Washington: The National Council on the Aging, Inc., 1975.

Lowry, Robert N. *Working with Homebound Adults in the Sunday School.* Nashville: Convention Press, 1977.

McClellan, Robert W. *Claiming a Frontier: Ministry and Older People.* Los Angeles: University of Southern California Press, 1977.

Mead, J. Earl. *Meditations from the Mountains.* (A cassette tape.) Nashville: Broadman Products, 1978.

Miller, Sarah Walton. *Drama for Senior Adults.* Nashville: Broadman Press, 1978.

Miller, Sarah Walton, and Medaris, Don. *Count on Us: A Musical for Senior Adults.* Nashville: Lighthearted Press, 1977.

Mission Action Group Guide: The Aging. Birmingham: Woman's Missionary Union of the Southern Baptist Convention, 1975.

Padula, Helen. *Developing Day Care for Older People.* Washington: The National Council on the Aging, Inc., 1975.

Prevost, Tom E. *Aging-Senior Impact: Handbook on Aging and Senior Adult Ministries.* Atlanta: Home Mission Board of the Southern Baptist Convention, 1976.

Publications List. (Offering helpful monographs on services to the elderly.) Write to The National Council on the Aging, Inc., 1828 L. Street, NW, Washington, D.C. 20036.

Pylant, Agnes. *God Talks with a Senior Adult.* (A cassette tape.) Nashville: Broadman Products, 1978.

Robb, Thomas Bradley. *The Bonus Years.* Valley Forge: Judson Press, 1968.

Schwartz, Arthur N., and Peterson, James A. *Introduction to Gerontology.* New York: Holt, Rinehart and Winston, 1979.

Sessoms, Robert. *52 Complete Recreation Programs for Senior Adults.* Nashville: Convention Press, 1979.

Sessoms, Robert. *150 Ideas for Activities with Senior Adults.* Nashville: Broadman Press, 1977.

Sessoms, Robert. *Senior Adult Mixers.* Nashville: Broadman Supplies, 1976.

Stagg. Frank. *Biblical Perspectives on Aging.* Athens, Georgia: National Interfaith Coalition on Aging, Inc., 1978.

Steen, John Warren. *Enlarge Your World.* Nashville: Broadman Press, 1978.

Tournier, Paul. *Learn to Grow Old.* New York: Harper & Row, Publishers, 1971.

Vickery, Florence E. *Creative Programming for Older Adults.* New York: Association Press, 1972.